THE ETHICAL EXECUTIVE

A TOP C.E.O.'S PROGRAM
for
SUCCESS WITH INTEGRITY
IN THE CORPORATE WORLD

by
DONALD V. SEIBERT
and
WILLIAM PROCTOR

CORNERSTONE LIBRARY

Published by Simon & Schuster, Inc.
New York

CORNERSTONE LIBRARY and colophon are registered trademarks of
Simon & Schuster, Inc.

10 9 8 7 6 5 4 3 2 1

Manufactured in the United States of America

Library of Congress Cataloging in Publication Data

Seibert, Donald V.,
    The ethical executive.

    1. Success in business. 2. Executive ability.
I. Proctor, William.   II. Title.
HF5386.S4158   1984   658.4'09   83-25247
ISBN: 0-346-12450-6

To the many JCPenney associates with whom I worked for thirty-six years. Our shared experiences are reflected in this book.

And to the many people I've met inside and outside business who give of themselves to help others.

CONTENTS

CONTENTS

FOREWORD

When a person has reached a certain level of achievement in any field, it sometimes seems rather easy to look back on the past and identify those qualities or circumstances that were important to later success. Yet, when you're in the midst of the daily challenges and pressures of life, the basic ingredients of success are often not evident at all. Such has been the case with me.

My forebears, who settled in German communities around Cincinnati, Ohio, in the nineteenth century, were hardworking people who made a living with their hands. My great-grandfather, who first settled in Newport, Kentucky, was a blacksmith by trade. His son Jacob, my grandfather, was also a blacksmith, but instead of forging horseshoes, he worked on streetcars. Eventually, he became Chief Blacksmith for the Cincinnati Railway Company.

Grandfather Jacob was probably physically the strongest person I've ever met — but his personal interests went well beyond activities that required mere brawn. For example, he liked to make simple toys for me and his other grandchildren. Also, he liked to play musical instruments and, as a result, started one of the earliest bands in Cincinnati.

Jacob's interest in using tools and making practical things apparently carried over to my father, Carl, who became a mechanical engineer after completing his education at the University of Cincinnati and the Ohio Mechanic Institute. In fact, my dad held hundreds of patents for items he had invented by the time he died. Also, he carried on the family musical tradition by playing at his church and directing the local orchestra. My mother, Minnie, had a creative flair with writing. Before she got married, she wrote scripts for radio shows and plays. After her marriage, she directed her activist inclinations toward community service, assistance to the poor, and church work in Hamilton, Ohio, where they eventually settled.

You might think, with all this diligence, energy, and variety of interests, that my family would have achieved significant financial success. But such was not the case. Things were fairly comfortable for us when I was born on August 17, 1923, and also when my siblings, the twins Carl Jr. and Jean, were born three years later. In those days, my father was an engineer in the Machine Tool Works in Hamilton, Ohio, and we had a fairly comfortable life. But then the Great Depression hit, and what material advancement we had made was kicked out from under us.

My father lost his engineering job, and we had to move to a third-floor, walk-up flat in the commercial section of Hamilton. Our new place was over a garage that repaired and vulcanized tires, and so the smell of melting rubber constantly wafted up to our quarters. My dad continued to tinker with his inventions, and some of them, such as a car-waxing machine he developed, had some financial promise. But he never managed to turn his ideas into an entrepreneurial bonanza. Consequently, we continued to live rather modestly, though happily, in and around Hamilton.

As for me, growing up in this sort of environment — with a father and grandfather who were skillful at making things, with an entrepreneurial spirit permeating the household, and with only a limited amount of family income — I naturally got interested in business. I tried quite a few jobs as a youngster, including a paper route; a printing business I started with a secondhand press; and even the publication of a weekly newspaper with a friend. Also, I put my family musical training to good use by taking a job several nights a week in a dance band as a saxophone and clarinet player. Later, I played the piano and sang in various professional groups.

Finally, while still a teenager, I decided to take a job in the retail business as a shoe salesman in a Hamilton department store. Although I didn't realize it at the time, this position was to be the type of work that "stuck" when I tried to decide on a career later in life. In short, I loved selling those shoes. Also, I was on commission, and so the more I sold, the more money I made. Some of the older, more seasoned salesmen taught me the fundamentals of selling; as a result, I made out pretty well for what was in effect a one-day job on the weekends.

Even with this wide job experience, when I entered the University of Cincinnati right after high school, I had no idea what I wanted to be. I began to study industrial design without any real sense of why I was doing it. Then, World War II intervened, and I enlisted in the Army Air Corps in 1942. This enabled me to put off any final decisions about the direction of my life. Over the next few years things started to come more into focus for me career-wise, in part because of increasing maturity and perhaps also because of the fact that I got married and acquired a greater sense of responsibility.

I met my wife-to-be, Verna, while I was in the service, and we immediately hit it off. The daughter of a career Navy man, she grew up in Binghamton, New York, became a nurse there, and then took a job in a doctor's office and hospital in Kearny, N.J. One night, toward the end of the war, Verna's cousin and the cousin's date invited her to go with them to a local restaurant. Verna was reluctant to go because she didn't have a date and was afraid she would be a "fifth wheel." But finally she consented, and when she and her two companions sat at their table, her cousin's date saw me across the room.

"Verna, I've got you a date," he said.

And indeed, he did. We went out for the next three nights, and I immediately proposed. After a two-year military courtship, we were married in Pennsylvania in 1945. Soon afterward when I was discharged from the service, I was an older and wiser young man, but still without a clear-cut career direction. With the passage of time and the arrival of our first child, however, I knew the time had come to make some long-term choices. I had reduced my options to two fields — either playing professionally in a band or retailing. After a brief experience with a band that fell apart in Chautauqua, New York, I decided to concentrate on retailing. In 1947, I took a job as a shoe salesman for a JCPenney store in Bradford, Pennsylvania. Of course, the Penney Company became my employer for the next thirty-six years.

Clearly, I had no overall plan at an early age to "move up" to a certain occupational position. In fact, even after I joined JCPenney, I just tried to do my best from day to day and year to year, without thinking too much about how far I expected to ascend on the many rungs of the corporate ladder that extended above me. I did have goals, but they were specific, short-term objectives that focused on accomplishing the immediate tasks before me. If anyone had told me that one day I would become the chief executive officer of my company, I might have been pleased at the compliment. But I wouldn't have bothered to let the thought linger in my mind for more than a few moments. I'm inclined to think that if I had always been looking at the top of the mountain, I would probably have stumbled much more often on the rocky lower ledges of daily business life.

What follows is in many ways a personal account of one man's movement upward through the challenges of an American corporate career. At the same time, I hope that some of my experiences and observations may be helpful to others who are somewhere on their own career climb. Throughout this book, I'll be touching on many subjects about which I in no way claim to be an expert. But I trust that the broad brush with which I describe many problems and challenges of a corporate career will serve as a reasonably useful guide for the average reader. Now, let's plunge into some of the details that make the experience of "moving up" in corporate America such an exciting and rewarding endeavor.

THE ETHICAL
EXECUTIVE

CHAPTER 1

IS THERE *an* EXECUTIVE PERSONALITY?

Suppose you are chosen by your company to interview several different people for a management position. In summary, their most memorable qualifications from their résumés look like this:

Candidate 1: A lawyer who has worked for the U.S. Justice Department. College and law degrees from top schools.

Candidate 2: A blue-collar worker, specializing in repair and maintenance jobs for a large communications corporation. High school education.

Candidate 3: A chemical engineer with on-the-job training in physically demanding oilfield work.

Candidate 4: A singer and saxophone player in a dance band, with some experience selling shoes. Some college education, no degrees.

If these were your major impressions of the résumés of the four candidates, which do you think you would be most likely to choose? Probably, in light of today's "common wisdom" about corporate leadership, you'd go for candidate 1—though perhaps you'd allow candidate 3 to stay in the running if the management job required some special technical expertise.

But in fact, *all four* of the people with these backgrounds have been elevated in recent years to the position of chairman or president of major American corporations! Also, I might add—and you should guess from the Foreword—that I am candidate 4, the singer and saxophone player with some background in selling shoes!

The point of this little exercise is not to suggest that your personal strategy for moving toward the top of a major corporation should necessarily involve saxophone-playing or blue-collar repair work. Rather, the lesson is that it's not helpful to be too concerned with stereotypes about what it takes to make it in business.

One of the reasons that there will probably always be a place in the highest echelons for those with backgrounds that don't fit any stereotype is that there is a growing recognition that variety in management can enhance a company's productivity. In other words, the more competent minds you have focusing on any given problem from every possible angle, the more likely you are to improve your overall efficiency and maximize your profits.

In this regard, much has been said and written in the past few years about how American business can learn from the "team" concepts of management employed by the Japanese. As *Business Week* has noted, we at the JCPenney Company have been relying for a long time on policies usually associated with the Japanese—such as an emphasis on employment security and nonadversarial relations with customers and employees. More recently, we've adopted, as *Business Week* puts it, "another quintessentially Japanese business concept: consensus management."

In brief, "consensus management," also called "team management" and "group management," refers to the practice of allowing a variety of executives to have an equal voice in most major company decisions. Sometimes, of course, the buck has to stop with one person. But more often, a decision can be made more effectively if several people with expertise and interest in a particular issue get to participate in the decision-making process. So our company, along with a growing number of other major corporations, likes to have a wide variety of good people with divergent backgrounds helping to make important judgments.

In our research into this area of team management, we have found that it's a relatively recent phenomenon in Japan. The Japanese picked it up from the United States from studies about how successful American companies manage their business. Before that, the Japanese were very autocratic in management. So they have taken an American idea and developed it to a much higher level. Now, ironically, we are trying to adapt it *back* to our culture, even though it originally developed in our system!

One illustration I like to use to encourage the consensus-management approach at JCPenney is to compare the human mind to a computer. If you accept the idea that the human brain is like a supercomputer, you can imagine thousands of human computers with an almost infinite amount of accumulated knowledge. Our objective is to tap this information resource as thoroughly as possible.

The primary difference between the human and the electronic computer is that the human computer can punch its own button. As a result, we need to recognize the fact that people must be trained to become self-starters so that they can "access" their own personal "computers." They must be motivated and pushed to become personally involved in the decision-making process.

All of this talk about the growing importance of team management and "human computers" is just another way of saying that there is no room at the top levels of corporation management for rigid stereotypes about what type of person can become a success at business. If you try to classify people, including yourself, too much—such as by saying, "I'm good with my hands," or "She is good with her brain"—you've missed something. You've written off an asset.

Every person is good with his brain in some way. Furthermore, many more individuals than you may realize are potentially good leaders in business. *You* may well be one of them—if you can just find your proper niche and develop the skills necessary to exercise effective executive leadership.

It's easy, then, to be misled by the stereotype of the cigar-chomping, foot-on-the-desk, overweight executive. It's also easy to be misled into believing that there is just one kind of résumé or background that can pave the way to success in business. That kind of popular notion just isn't true.

Remember my own background as candidate 4: The main thing I had going for me—and this was a quality which could only be hinted at in a résumé or an initial interview—was that I had learned how to be a good shoe salesman. And quite frankly, I *knew* I was good. My attitude helped me get the job, and that spark of self-confidence in an otherwise unexceptional set of credentials proved enough to build on in the early stages of my career.

Precisely the same principle applies to you. You may feel you have many things going against you as far as a business career is concerned. But with the right attitude and proper motivation, you may actually have a much better chance of moving up in the business world than you realize.

To enhance your self-confidence, just remember that the team concept of management, with its stress on diversity of backgrounds in decision-making, is growing in importance. So your special job and educational history, which you may think will seem strange or detrimental to others, may actually catch the imagination of an interviewer who is looking for variety.

Also, keep in mind that regardless of the team-management approach, the popular stereotypes of senior executives are just that and nothing more—stereotypes. You may have heard, for example, that the top slots in the business world are reserved for hard-nosed individuals who are so tough they are a breed apart from humanity in general, and from you in particular. Actually, though, most of the stereotypes that have made people hesitant about embarking on a corporate career are simply inaccurate.

For instance, take the image of the selfish, overly aggressive executive who is monomaniacal on the subject of company profits. Although this may reflect some actual person in some very real corporation, I must say, I've never met him. Yet that stereotype and similar clichés persist in the popular mind and media.

I'm reminded of a review in the *New York Daily News* of the movie *The Electric Horseman*, which starred Robert Redford and Jane Fonda. The reviewer noted, "And once more Fonda's main opposition comes from white-collar villains, the corporation president (played with comic ruthlessness by a sleek-looking John Saxon) and his fawning executive staff."

As I said, the ruthless white-collar villain with his fawning executive staff may exist somewhere, but I've never run into him. That type of person always seems to get weeded out in the movement toward the top. Believe it or not, the people you're most likely to run into at the upper levels of the nation's corporations are for the most part actually more concerned with creative marketing ideas and the manufacture of good products than they are with playing the game of internal corporate politics.

You may also have read that the typical upwardly mobile young executive knows how to manipulate people and situations and is usually preoccupied with certain outward status symbols, such as clothes, office furnishings, and the like. But the *real* people I want you to meet through the examples and principles in this book—the top-level executives of big national corporations—are as diverse as the people with whom you grew up and now associate.

They are as likely to be soft-spoken and retiring as they are to be extroverts with a military command voice and jutting jaw. Of course, they *do* tend to have some things in common. For example, they work hard; they are competitive; they set high standards for themselves. But they are also, for the most part, highly individualistic and more sensitive to others than you might expect.

Now, I want to try to guide you past the clichés and stereotypes and introduce you to what people at the top levels are actually like and what concrete steps will improve your chances to join them. But let me offer one word of caution at the outset: I don't want to give you the impression that I "know it all," because I don't. I'm not an expert in personnel, computers, or many other specialized areas. As I've moved up the corporate ladder, however, I have developed an overview and a general "feel" for the skills and qualities I believe are important for your success. It's these fundamental principles of success that I want to share with you.

Nothing is ever guaranteed, but the important thing for you to know is that you may be as capable of making it up there as anyone. The world of business is constantly looking for those with executive potential. You may be one. Now, let's examine exactly what's involved in moving up.

CHAPTER 2

DO YOU HAVE WHAT IT TAKES *to* MAKE IT *in* BUSINESS?

You may be suited for a successful business career—but the main thing holding you back could be your own failure to realize you are executive material. Often, those with the greatest potential miss out on an exciting business experience because their minds are filled with mistaken notions about what it takes to make it successfully and happily to the upper levels of management.

Some avoid the business world because they think you have to be a tall, white, Anglo-Saxon Protestant male to move up. Others assume you have to be a glib back-slapper, or operate a little dishonestly, or stifle your creativity and individuality, or run over people to get promotions. So they decide, "If I have to compromise my principles that way, I'll just stay out of the rat race!"

These attitudes are unfortunate, because they are based on faulty information. Men and women who represent almost every personality type and who come from every ethnic and social group are becoming successful in business these days—and they are doing it without compromising their creativity or moral principles one whit.

Also, they come from almost every educational background imaginable. There are people in the upper echelons of the nation's major corporations who started out as engineers, lawyers, accountants, salesmen—even musicians, like me.

The point I want to make here is this: There is almost no field or background that will disqualify you for a business career. The important thing is that you take some of those talents, skills, and aptitudes you've developed at school or another job and apply them wholeheartedly to the requirements of the business field you choose.

One field which might seem to be unfertile ground for producing a corporate executive is research science. But Carl Djerassi, who is popularly known as the "father of the birth-control pill," moved quite naturally from success in the laboratory to additional responsibilities in the top spot at the Zoecon Corporation. Zoecon was established by Syntex, a pharmaceutical company, to study insecticides and was recently grossing about $45 million worth of business each year.

How did Dr. Djerassi, an individual who doesn't fit most of the popular executive stereotypes, make this successful move into business while other research scientists are still locked in their labs?

There are many features in this scientist's personality which are often connected with business success. For one thing, he is incredibly energetic and works harder than the average person. At one point in his career, he combined research responsibilities in Mexico and a teaching load at Wayne State University in Detroit. He was actually so pressed for time he had to conduct classes with his students during taxi rides to the Detroit airport. And the workload he imposes on himself hasn't let up since he took over as the head of Zoecon. In addition to his corporate responsibilities, he holds down a post as professor of chemistry at Stanford University and finds time to write books on his work for the general public.

But Dr. Djerassi is not a typical executive, just as I am not. In fact, you might say there is no such thing as a typical executive. The mold for upward mobility seems to have been made a little differently for each individual, and it's frequently in the unique qualities and the distinctive idiosyncrasies that the key to success for each person may be found.

Still, business pundits continue to look for a common core of characteristics that identify the high-potential worker in American corporations. And to some extent they have succeeded in isolating a number of personality types and individual qualities that are common to many company leaders. One study by a New York recruiting firm, Russell Reynolds Associates Inc., reported that *growth potential*—which was defined as "leadership qualities and a capacity to move into new and expanded responsibilities"—was listed as important by 94 percent of the more than one thousand large corporations surveyed. *Creativity* was the second most frequently listed characteristic of an executive, rated as important by 64 percent of the companies.

Others have attempted to argue that a person's family and social background are the key factors in success. For example, Richard H. deLone, in his *Small Futures: Children, Inequality and the Limits of Liberal Reform*, reported that there's a good chance you family's social and economic status will determine the limits of your own potential in business and life. DeLone's research, which was sponsored by the Carnegie Council on Children, reveals that only one man in five moves above his father's social standing.

There is probably a great deal of validity in these findings, but let me offer one word of caution: You can't plan your life and your career around statistical summaries and probabilities. You are an individual, a unique person with very special qualities and potential which, when channeled properly, can *definitely* result in some advancement in business.

But do you also have what it takes to make it as an *executive* in business?

The answer to this question may well be yes. You may be surprised to discover that you have certain basic executive strengths that have remained latent and unrecognized in the past. One of the things I hope to do in the following pages is to help you find those strong points and understand how they can be developed to further your career.

In my more than thirty years of business experience, I have identified ten key attributes, each of which can take you one step closer to the upper executive levels in your company. You'll note that each of these qualities is prefaced by the word "willingness." The reason for this is that the decisive factor in achieving success is having both the desire to improve yourself and also the persistence to turn your weaknesses into strengths.

Now, take a look at these ten qualities and see how you measure up personally to each of them:

1. Willingness to continue your formal education.

I don't think it's absolutely necessary to have a graduate degree or even a college degree to succeed in life. But in today's economy a college degree *has* become almost a prerequisite for entry into the world of business management. And an appropriate graduate degree, such as a master's in business administration, can at the very least give you a definite short-term advantage.

You'll enter the corporation at a higher rate of pay, and according to some recent studies, you may also find you retain a certain advantage as you move up the corporate ladder. One survey conducted by the UCLA Graduate School of Management and Korn/Ferry International showed that 43 percent of the 1,700 top-level executives polled had graduate degrees. Of those with post graduate diplomas, 41 percent had M.B.A. degrees and 26 percent had law degrees, and nearly 20 percent had earned their graduate degrees at Harvard.

But I wouldn't want to give you a distorted or simplistic picture of the significance of an M.B.A. or another graduate degree. Statistics can teach us only so much. In the last analysis, you have to approach your education with an eye to the specific requirements of specific companies. Some companies these days *require* management candidates to have an M.B.A. But other companies regard advanced degrees as only optional.

No matter what your company's minimum educational requirements may be, though, any additional education that makes you a better-informed worker can only enhance your upward movement. There are many helpful courses in local colleges, such as computer programming for nonprofessionals and finance for nonfinancial managers. These can greatly improve your job performance and general business knowledge, and in larger corporations you'll find the company will often foot the bill for extra courses you may want to take. The more you take advantage of opportunities like this, the better will be your chances for moving toward the upper management level.

2. Willingness to continue your informal education.

I'm always favorably impressed by middle-level executives and managers who show their intellectual curiosity by reading extensively and seeking out helpful business seminars which may not even award academic credits.

In the first place, extra reading and informal study are worthwhile to show your boss you have an active mind and a breadth of knowledge at your disposal in any type of conversation. In other words, anything that will improve your ability to communicate can only work to your advantage on the job, because this skill will almost certainly help you gain new respect and recognition from your peers and superiors.

It's interesting to note in this regard a finding by the Human Engineering Laboratory of the Johnson O'Connor Research Foundation in New York City. According to an article on the research of the laboratory in *Publishers Weekly*, "Successful people in every line of endeavor share one thing in common—and often only one—a high vocabulary." Of those tested, top business executives generally register the highest scores, with editors, writers, and college professors following them in that order. The report concludes: "The hundreds of thousands of tests administered by Johnson O'Connor have shown this to be true: a person with a high vocabulary may not necessarily succeed, but a person with a low vocabulary practically never succeeds."

I can't think of a better way to improve your vocabulary and other communications skills than through regular outside reading. But it's a sad fact that too many people in business don't read important best-sellers or business books, and others don't even read the newspaper very carefully. If you decide to apply yourself in these areas you'll not only enjoy considerable self-satisfaction, but you'll also discover there are uses of this outside information on your job which you may never have dreamed existed.

For example, top executives have sometimes learned the hard way that they can put themselves at a serious disadvantage if they don't keep up to date on business and social trends. Suppose that you've been asked by your boss to participate in a study-advisory group that must come up with a recommendation on the likely impact on your business of a "value-added tax." It would be highly advisable, both for the good of your company and also for the future of your own career, for you to walk into such a meeting *only* after having thoroughly prepared yourself through a considerable amount of background study and reading.

I've actually known aspiring junior executives who attend a session like this, and the first words out of their mouths are, in effect, "What's a value-added tax, anyway?" That's certainly the perfect approach to take if you want to be useless in the discussion and also deal your career a setback.

But not many would be so completely negligent in their responsibilities. Most would at least read the briefing papers their company put out on the subject, perhaps make a few notes in the margins, and then go in with at least some notion of what the conversation is going to involve. Then, if they're fairly good talkers, they may find they can "wing it" during the session and may even be able to make a few helpful contributions.

But the very high achiever, the junior executive or middle manager who is the best candidate for higher office, will do considerably more. He'll pay a visit to the local library, where he will perhaps first check a standard economic dictionary, like the Sloan-Zurcher *Dictionary of Economics*, or the *McGraw-Hill Dictionary of Modern Economics*. In those volumes he would learn that a value-added tax (or VAT) is a "tax levied at all levels of manufacture, processing, and distribution, but based only on the amount a particular level adds to the price." These basic reference books would also reveal that the VAT has been used in France and elsewhere in the European Economic Community.

Then the topflight young businessperson would check more recent news about the VAT by going through the guides to periodical literature. There he might find back articles in the *Wall Street Journal, Fortune,* and other business publications on all the implications of the tax. Another possible source of helpful information would be the tax department in his own corporation.

As a result of his extensive research, this person will go into that meeting with not only a good basic definition of a value-added tax, but also many other details about it—such as how it has worked in other parts of the world, the effect of the tax on companies similar to the home company, and views of other industry leaders and tax experts on the pros and cons of the tax.

Maintaining a good image and reputation for yourself may be a side effect of thorough preparation for a business session like this. But an even more central concern is what you can do, in concrete terms, to provide tangible help for your company. If your contributions to such a study group can assist your bosses in making the right decisions—and consequently enable your company to take a more profitable path—you'll begin to realize the maximum personal dividends from your informal study efforts.

3. Willingness to operate at maximum capacity, with minimum compulsion.

If you hope to make it to the upper levels of management in your company, you have to do more than just work hard, and also you have to go beyond merely doing your best. I'm not saying you have to be superhuman or put in twenty hours a day to be successful. But it is necessary to continue to test the limits of just what constitutes "hard work" and "your best" in your life.

You'll most likely also find that those above you in the corporate hierarchy are constantly watching and evaluating you to see just how dedicated you are to maintaining a high level of productivity—because this is a subject that is important in the minds of top-level executives. In one recent survey of 782 chief executives conducted by the Gallup Poll and the *Wall Street Journal*, "industriousness" was one of the major qualities that was cited as important to advancement in large, medium-sized, and small firms.

I've felt on a number of occasions that I was working extremely hard. But then, as I "fine-tuned" my approach to concentration, I learned later that I had actually been operating at a level of intensity well short of my maximum capacity. Similarly, the level I might have considered "my best" at one point often became something less than my best as I increased my level of personal productivity.

I believe that to work at maximum capacity means to achieve a quality of performance that exceeds, even if ever so slightly, the level of excellence once achieved in the past. It's a matter of sweeping aside preconceptions about the limits you've set in the past for your work, and trying to remain free and flexible enough to push back those limits to new definitions of your own personal "maximum capacity."

But there's a danger in trying to achieve your maximum capacity on the job, and that's why I've included that phrase "with minimum compulsion" in stating this principle. Most people who want to achieve big things in life tend to go overboard at one time or another. They want to do a good job so badly—a job that will outshine all others—that they get compulsive about it. They become rigid perfectionists, and this trap may actually do them more harm than good in their effort to move up in their corporation.

So at this point I'd like to be sure all the perfectionists among us install some safety valves in their approach to work. For example, I think many competent people who have a shot at making it to senior levels tend to be tempted to stick with a job just a little too long, in an effort to put that final veneer of perfection on their work product. Frequently, staying with a project a little longer than the average person *can* make the difference between a mediocre and a superior performance. But sometimes, hanging on to a task even beyond the superior stage, in a conscious or subconscious effort to make it perfect, can be counterproductive.

I know some people who almost become monomaniacs on certain tasks, and the result is that their other work suffers. They're always running out of time, they work unnecessarily long hours, and their energies are sapped through anxieties that arise from never feeling on top of all their responsibilities. My advice to you, if you suffer from the malady of perfectionism, would be this: Work at full steam, but know when to ease back on the throttle! If you're unable to draw the line between hard work and compulsive work, you'll burn yourself out long before you reach your maximum capacity in the total array of responsibilities and jobs that confront you.

Of course, even if you master your perfectionist tendencies, it's still not at all easy to do a maximum-capacity job on all your projects. To reach this level, it's likely you'll have to put in more hours and more intense concentration than the next guy. That may not be particularly good news, but it's a fact.

As an illustration, in the Korn/Ferry executive survey, one question was: "If you could name a single factor that was most significant in bringing about your success, what would it be?" The number-one response mentioned by those polled was "hard work." Or, as one of the interviewees put it, "hard work and lots of it!"

Those executives questioned in that study were also asked to list "traits that enhance executive success," and the most common answer, mentioned by 73.7 percent of the business leaders, was "concern for results." And believe me, it's impossible to get consistently good results without plenty of mental elbow grease!

But let me put on the brakes for a moment. In doing all this cheerleading for hard work, I'm not trying to turn you into a corporate automaton, a work machine with no time to enjoy life. I just want to encourage you to be *willing* to throw yourself so completely into a business career that you give yourself every opportunity to make that job an exciting adventure rather than a daily dose of drudgery.

Also, in encouraging you to work up to your maximum capacity I don't want to suggest that you set out to ignore your family and friends and become a classic "workaholic," who subordinates all other values to his occupation. When I'm in New York, I try to save as many evenings for my family as I can, because I believe they are that important. But even with these qualifications, I do want to try to build a fire under you so you'll go the extra mile and make the extra effort that will enhance your chances for bigger and better things.

4. Willingness to be sociable.

Despite certain popular stereotypes, it isn't necessary to be the life of the party or an aggressive extravert to advance in business. All that's required is that you be willing to be genuine with others—and also that you develop a special knack for getting along well with them. The survey of the nation's chief executives by the Gallup Poll and the *Wall Street Journal* disclosed that one-third of the top corporate officers, responding from all sizes of firms, believed that "ability to get along with others" is a major key to advancement and promotion.

Perhaps you don't like to tell jokes or slap backs, but you may enjoy serious conversation about the theater or world events. Or you may just like to *listen* to what others want to talk about. If so, then don't force yourself to become something you're not. The important thing is to be sincere and pleasant, and you'll be well on your way toward developing the kind of personality that goes with success in business.

I know chief executive officers who are soft-spoken and seem almost shy in their dealings with others. The room doesn't light up nor does an orchestra start playing when they walk through a door. But if you sit down and talk with one of them for a while, you find you're in the company of a person who is exceptionally well informed and who can communicate his or her ideas in a pleasant, interesting way.

In fact, the "shy" executive may actually end up dominating the conversation, but that's because his personality grows on you and surrounds you with a certain force of character. He rarely knocks you off your feet at the outset. But he often does have a genuine interest in people, a desire to listen to them, and an ability to get a point across in such a way that you just like being around him. These are the very qualities which turn out to be some of the most important in helping an executive do his job well and understand what makes those under him tick.

5. Willingness to compete for first place.

Some people are put off by the idea of competition in business because it may conjure up images of cutthroat struggles with other people, backstabbing your best friend, or giving free rein to some sort of "killer instinct."

Actually, though, that's not at all what competition should mean in the business world. The most successful people I know aren't obsessed with beating out the other person and stepping on others' heads to get to the top. Their motivation, instead, is to do such a good job at their assigned tasks that they come to be regarded as first in a fast field of excellent talent. In fact, the better your competitors do, the better it makes you look if you win first place. And the ultimate goal in any business is to assemble the best-trained, most highly motivated team in the industry so that as a group you can *all* become first in the marketplace.

It's interesting, by the way, to examine the Latin root of the word "compete" to help in understanding what the concept should mean today. The Latin source word is *competere*, which means, among other things, "to come together, agree, be suitable, belong, compete for."

There's nothing in this derivation that would even remotely suggest a "killer instinct" or a need to humiliate or destroy your opponent. Rather, it carries the idea of joining together in a friendly way with other people and then moving jointly toward the same goal— such as putting out a top-notch piece of work for the company.

In the last analysis, of course, one person, or a small group of people, have to "win" in the sense that they do a superior job and move up to a higher level of management. But in the long run, the right approach to competition should mean that everybody is better off just for having run the race.

Take the weekend tennis player, for example. I love to play tennis and try to play at least once a week. For a guy in his fifties, I guess I might be considered a fairly good player, and I do very much like to win every time I get out on the courts. But needless to say, I *don't* always win. I want to win and even expect to win because that enhances the fun and excitement of the game. But when I lose, I just shake the winner's hand, try to feel grateful for the opportunity to have injected a little more action and exercise into my life, and begin to go over my mistakes so that I'll have a better chance of being the one on top next time.

At whatever level you play tennis or any other sport —whether hacker or professional—there's always room for improvement. Losing pro football teams can always learn by reviewing old game films and trying to understand how to correct their mistakes. Their main goal is to win, but the best clubs profit by their losses—and the players on these teams don't have any opportunity to experience a win or learn from a loss unless they compete.

Your approach to competition at every level of business should be similar. Expect to enjoy the process of doing a good job on the tasks assigned to you. Strive to be the very best at what you're doing. But if somebody else beats you out, don't allow yourself to develop a loser's mentality: Evaluate your performance and see ways you can improve so you'll be the one promoted next time around.

6. Willingness to take risks on your own creativity.

To some people, it may seem totally incongruous to use words like "risk" and "creativity" when talking about a big corporation. Risk may appear to be an appropriate concept to apply to the entrepreneur, and creativity is almost always the first thing that comes to mind when you think of an artist. But a corporation employee?

Now, I'm not trying to strain your credulity, but actually, coming up with creative ideas and then being willing to take calculated risks on them is a key quality for the individual who wants to move up in any big corporation. As an illustration of this quality, I'm reminded of an innovative program for senior citizens that was initiated at one of the nation's major urban banks. A young female bank manager—call her Marsha—gradually developed a strong sense of mission to do something for older people who often seemed trapped in their small apartments. They were frequent targets of crime and had few opportunities to get out and participate safely in various kinds of recreation. From the viewpoint of the woman's bank, these older people were potential customers, but they had largely been written off as lost causes because it was too hard to get them out of their apartments and into the lines at the tellers' windows.

So Marsha sat down at home for a couple of evenings and came up with a bank-sponsored recreational and service program for senior citizens, which would not only help the older people enjoy life more but also had the potential of developing some new customers. She then submitted her proposal to her boss.

In so doing, she automatically introduced some risks — but perhaps not quite the serious kind of risks you might expect. Every time you exercise your creativity in a business situation and try to get your company to accept a new idea, you may *imagine* certain risks or contingencies that aren't really risks at all. For example, you may worry, "If they accept my idea and it's invalid for some reason I can't foresee right now, my company may lose a lot of money and I'll get all the blame!"

But the chances are that this will never happen, especially not in a large corporation. You see, in a sizable organization, major decisions almost always have to be shaped, "fine-tuned," and approved by several people or committees. So there are usually a number of "co-authors" of any new project who must take the credit or blame when the final results come in.

In other words, the risk you'll typically run is only that you may be one of several people linked to a failure; you won't bear the whole brunt of it. So it's important not to be timid about presenting your ideas to your superiors. Even if the concept falls flat, you won't be the only one who is held responsible. And if you do fail to put forward a good idea just because you're timid about the possibility of being associated with a marginal program or a real failure, your company will suffer in the long run, and you'll never get the opportunity to show just how creative you can be.

As for Marsha, after some initial skepticism, her proposal was approved as a formal bank project. But far from being a failure, it became one of the most exciting company programs that had come along in years. One sign of the degree of success was that before long, similar projects began to spring up in competitor banks. It soon became evident that Marsha's risk-taking venture was going to pay dividends for the bank as a whole, and for her personally as well.

The safe way of operating in this situation would have been for both Marsha and her boss to have reacted negatively to embarking on any sort of project that seemed out of the ordinary. But they had researched the program and thought through all the angles, and they held their ground—even when, at one point, some top-level executives questioned the wisdom of the proposal. And their courage and perseverance paid off with a successful project. This sort of approach to risk-taking can only work to your benefit when the time comes for you to be considered for a promotion.

7. Willingness to be self-confident.

I'm convinced that the main reason most people fall short of their potential, not just in business but in all life's activities, is that they have never taken the time to develop some self-confidence. This quality is truly one which you have to be *willing* to acquire, or you'll never get it.

I have known many men and women who, on paper, looked as though they should have become shooting stars in their careers. But then something seemed to go wrong. Perhaps they saw someone on their level who seemed to be doing a better job on most things than they were, and this discouraged them. Or maybe they fell short a couple of times in tasks that were assigned to them and then gave up.

In such situations, the result is often that highly capable people who have a few imperfections, as we all do, begin to sell themselves short. They focus on their weaknesses rather than their strengths. They begin to assume that they are inferior to their peers, and whatever natural self-confidence they may have had begins to ebb away.

In my own work experience, I've come to the conclusion that all self-confidence, other than that which is a deeply grained inherited or family-conditioned trait, stems from three major sets of factors: (1) solid study and preparation, (2) persistence and practice, and (3) a *willingness* to be self-confident and not be content with failure.

To illustrate this idea, let me give you a personal example from my experience at JCPenney. I found I was doing fairly well and feeling quite comfortable in my upward movement in the company until I started having to give increasing numbers of public speeches and other presentations before large groups. I'm not a natural public person, and I was absolutely terrified the first few times I gave business talks. As a matter of fact, it took me ten or fifteen years to feel comfortable with public speaking before big groups.

I had never had much of a problem speaking extemporaneously in a small group on a subject I knew well. But if you expanded the group beyond eight or ten people and there were strangers present who I suspected might be more expert than I on the subject matter, I would start to get more nervous. The larger the group would get, the shakier my knees would become—until I found I could hardly stand up when I was asked one year to give my first "scripted" talk to a Penney convention.

When I stepped up to the lectern on that occasion, the lights went down, and a bright spotlight zeroed in on me. The audience was dead quiet except for the tinkling of a few coffee cups, and I was sure they could hear or see my heart pounding as I began reading my script.

Somehow, I managed to get through the talk and returned to my chair without collapsing on the way, but I knew I had to do something about this fear of speaking. And it's not even that anyone else knew how uncomfortable I was feeling. As a matter of fact, I received quite a few compliments on how well my speech had gone. The real problem was how I felt inside, and also how the excessive tension and discomfort drained my energies from other responsibilities and robbed me of the joy of doing a good job behind the podium.

So even though I suspected the image I was projecting to my audiences wasn't quite as bad as I imagined, I also knew I could be doing a much better job if only I had more confidence in myself. The important thing at this stage was that I was *willing* to do something about my deficiencies. As a result, I decided to make an appointment with a physician I knew to see if he could do anything about my nervousness.

He explained that my system automatically prepared my body to defend itself against outside threats, as a kind of animal instinct. So the excitement of facing a large audience triggered a surge of adrenaline, which was more than my body could absorb, since I wasn't moving about vigorously enough on the platform to use it up.

The doctor said, "You'd be in great shape to go a two-minute round in boxing, and that would quickly take care of that extra surge of energy. But you're not as well prepared to stand still behind a podium and deliver a talk. So find some ways to move around up there!"

His advice made sense, so I began to look for places in my speeches that would give me an excuse to pace about or gesture broadly. I started marking up my scripts on almost every page with a little note or cartoon to remind me of a spot where I could insert an ad-lib or a personal story. Then, when I found myself getting shaky, I would stop reading my script, step around to the side of the podium and say, "This reminds me of something I experienced last week . . ."

It took me a few speeches before I felt comfortable moving away from my prepared text and then back into it. But before long, I found that this gimmick I had developed was giving me greater control over my nervousness before large crowds. I've since had an opportunity to share this insight with others who have had problems with public speaking, and one of my colleagues actually commented, "You know, I always thought those little stories you told were the best part of your talks!"

But let me repeat: Success and self-confidence in this area didn't come overnight. It really did take me ten to fifteen years before I finally felt comfortable delivering prepared speeches before large groups. In the process, I learned that the more I knew about a subject and the more I practiced speaking, the more self-confidence I developed.

Defined in its simplest terms, self-confidence is nothing more than a feeling that you can do an acceptable job on something. You may not be at all confident about your ability to fix a drippy faucet or cook a meal when your spouse is sick. But think about it for a moment: You can read, and there's a how-to book on almost everything in the world these days. You can pick up a home-maintenance book or a simple cookbook and do a good job on tasks you never thought you were capable of doing. It's just a matter of getting some information and trying to put it into effect a few times.

Confidence in business comes about in precisely the same way. You get as much information as you can, and then you apply it intelligently. The more you use this new knowledge, the more comfortable you become—and the more your self-confidence grows.

But let me offer one word of caution at this point as you launch your quest for self-confidence: It's important to reach and stretch for a sense of inner certainty, but don't *over*reach. The self-confidence you attain should be rooted in a realistic understanding of your abilities, and not in some sort of groundless positive thinking.

In the area of speaking before business groups, for example, I'm always careful to make it clear at the outset exactly what I know *and* what I don't know. I certainly try to avoid the trap of beginning with an apology for all the things I don't know, because that can make a person look weak and uncertain, and his presentation will suffer accordingly. But at the same time, I avoid pretending to know things I don't know.

One illustration of this principle involved a talk I gave on store construction to a group which included a number of architects. I made it clear at the outset that I didn't have all the technical knowledge about buildings and structures that they had. But at the same time, I knew I had done my homework and I was aware I understood more about how a Penney store operated than they did. I approached the buildings from the way the customers would see them, the way the products were presented, and the techniques required to make the store show a profit. So I stressed my own special areas of knowledge and used the question-and-answer sessions afterward to find ways to combine my special knowledge with theirs.

The result was that I projected confidence about those things I knew well, but I was also straightforward about the limits of my knowledge. This kind of honesty produces a *realistic* self-confidence, which blossoms and flourishes when it's given a fertile field in which to grow in a person's life.

8. Willingness to communicate openly with your superiors.

This point is related to what has already been mentioned about self-confidence, but something more needs to be said. To put it directly, you need to promote yourself if you hope to make it as an executive—at least that's what is indicated by the findings of Henchey & Company, a New York recruiting firm. A survey by this organization revealed that 83 percent of fired executives "didn't aggressively call their superiors' attention to their achievements." They chose to sit back and wait to be recognized; but obviously, that approach didn't work.

It's important to speak up and let your views be known, even if you occasionally get shot down. Your boss can't read your mind, and frequently he has so many other things vying for his attention that your ideas and accomplishments may be overlooked if you don't point them out.

I'm certainly not suggesting that you be overly pushy. But there are times when you must take the initiative to keep lines of communication open with your superiors. For example, it's essential to participate openly in conferences and brainstorming sessions. Your boss always has an ear cocked for ideas and is interested in anyone who can bring something new to problem-solving or inject an incisive word or good judgment into a conversation.

But don't wait for a completely original idea to pop into your mind before you contribute something. I'm not even sure there *are* any original ideas anymore. There are so many business meetings where a person will come up with what seems to be a unique concept, and three or four colleagues may even confirm its seeming originality. But then a fifth person will come along and say, "Oh, so-and-so suggested that in the Acme Company when I was with them four years ago. And then there was another person with the same idea in the Widget Corporation."

Just that an idea isn't completely new or original, however, doesn't necessarily mean it's not creative or important. Your observation may just be incomplete. But when it's combined with the ideas of others, you may find you've made a substantial contribution to a new concept that can dramatically increase the profit-making potential of your company.

Group discussions become particularly important as you move higher in your organization, because there is a special dynamic in putting people together in the same room to discuss a topic. Often the final product isn't the result of just one individual's idea. But your concept or some other person's may have been the catalyst that sparked the formation of the final decision.

Good ideas mean money in business, and the more ways you can participate in generating and communicating them to your superiors, the stronger your position in the company will be. I was once asked at an international business conference in Tokyo, "Is it really worth spending all this money to travel here and talk?"

My response: "If you go away from this meeting with only one idea you can use, it's worth the price."

That's the kind of premium I place on getting ideas and sharing them aggressively with your colleagues.

I know it's sometimes difficult for many people, and especially for those in the early stages of their careers, to swallow their fears and express themselves openly in the presence of their superiors. You may feel you can't speak well enough, or you may suspect your idea isn't really all that good. "So why take a chance of making myself look foolish?" you say.

The reason is that you really won't be "taking a chance" if you try a contribution, because in the long run you have very little to lose and everything to gain. It's important to participate fully in order to be recognized fully in your peer group and by your bosses. Also, if you're too timid, you'll find yourself missing out on the excitement of give-and-take encounters with your colleagues. As in anything else, the more practice you get in expressing yourself, the more effective you'll be in future meetings.

There's an old saying, "The way to get ahead is to keep your head down." But at the very least, that's misleading. In fact, the best way to get ahead is to keep your head *up*, even if you expose yourself to a few potshots from time to time. You have a great deal more to lose by playing the low-profile wallflower in brainstorming sessions and other encounters with your bosses than you do by being willing to take a few chances. Let your superiors know what you think, and in a casual, tactful way, inform them about what you've done. The results can work only to your benefit.

9. Willingness to laugh during business hours.

A business career certainly involves *serious* business. But the person who takes himself and his work too seriously is at a disadvantage. I'm not suggesting that you should take your responsibilities in business lightly, but most of the people I know at the top have a great sense of humor. They can laugh in even grim situations.

As for me, I would be very depressed if I focused exclusively on all the bad things that happen in the world and national economy. I'd continually be preoccupied with all the negative news, such as inflation rates, wars, and unemployment. With this attitude, it would be quite possible to become a total business basket case.

I can't give you lessons on how to get a sense of humor if you don't already have one. All I'm saying is that if you *do* have a funny side to your nature, don't suppress it the minute you walk into a business meeting or boardroom. Even the worst situations somehow become more bearable if somebody injects a quip or humorous comment. It's genuinely uplifting to be around people who are capable of seeing something amusing in an otherwise bleak report.

This is certainly not to say that you should try to turn everything into a joke. The humor has to be appropriate to the situation—you can't give the impression that you're unconcerned about the difficulty or disaster that may be confronting your company. Also, you don't have to have a constantly ready string of jokes or try to become the company comic. But a quick smile or light comment at the right moment can act as a catalyst to put problems into perspective and help everyone else relax and get down to the job at hand. Humor is the best antidote I know for stress.

10. Willingness to settle on a comprehensive value system.

In a way, this final executive quality should have been put first, because it's so important to your ability to move up in a corporation. I'm sure most people outside the management field never consider the idea that it may be essential in business to develop a broad set of values that encompasses more than just the profit motive.

There are those who believe that ambition in business is the antithesis of a truly mature spiritual commitment or high ethical values. Yet in the survey conducted by the Gallup Poll and the *Wall Street Journal*, the chief executives in the largest firms most often put "integrity" at the very top of their list as the trait they thought was most important to promotion.

I consider the spiritual foundations of an executive's life—and the integrity and other character traits associated with a firm set of moral values—to be so important to success that I know I can't begin to cover the topic in a few paragraphs. So I'm going to devote the next chapter to this subject.

Before we move on, though, let me emphasize again one key point about each of these basic qualities that a person needs for success. It's not necessary for you actually to possess all these qualities right now, or before you make a serious attempt to succeed in business. All that's necessary is that you be *willing to develop* those qualities.

And this willingness presupposes that you won't give up even if you find you have to spend some extra time working on your educational background, or self-confidence, or competitive instincts, or whatever. Actually, part of the fun of moving up in business is seeing yourself get stronger and stronger in areas where you start off weak. As I've told you, public speaking was very difficult for me when I first began giving presentations before groups, and there were many other skills and qualities I lacked. You'll see what I'm talking about as I share some of my other personal "executive confessions" with you throughout this book.

If I've learned nothing else during the past three decades in the business world, I have come to understand two basic truths about success:

—You have to tackle your weak spots with a positive, open attitude that says, "I really want to turn this weakness into a strength, and I believe I can do it!"

—You have to be persistent about overcoming those weaknesses—so persistent, in fact, that you're willing to put in years, if need be, to correct a deficiency.

And part of the impetus and inner stamina to wrestle for long periods with personal weaknesses comes from that final executive quality that I mentioned—a willingness to settle on a comprehensive philosophy of life.

CHAPTER 3

The **PRIMARY PRINCIPLE:**
Defining Your Personal Values

As we move into this discussion of spiritual and moral commitments, I feel in a way as though I'm walking on eggshells, because it's so easy to be misunderstood. But I consider the ideas involved here to be so important that I'm willing to take a few risks to get the point across.

First, let's settle on some basic definitions. The "primary principle" we'll be exploring can be stated this way: If you want to succeed, it's extremely important to settle as soon as possible on some coherent, comprehensive set of personal values.

But in stating this principle, I'm not trying to argue that you should attempt to acquire such a set of values, which may be rooted in a firm religious faith or philosophical position, merely for the pragmatic reason of making it to the top levels in business. In the first place, I believe an authentic spiritual faith will certainly help you in your rise, but it won't by any means assure you of success. During one of my first jobs as a young man, I worked as a drill-press operator. In that capacity I met a number of people who started *and finished* their careers in hard labor—and their religious faith was at least equal to any I've encountered before or since.

Secondly, a common feature of most genuine philosophical commitments is that by definition they encompass a person's whole life and not just the hours spent at the office. So in this chapter we'll focus on only a small piece of the "spiritual pie," so to speak. I have no intention of trying to impose some sort of systematic theology on you. Instead, I just want to share some personal thoughts and observations about how a mature philosophy of life can help you relate more meaningfully to the business world.

Let me suggest five ways:

• **A personal philosophy of life provides a sense of perspective on what's important in life.** I've seen many highly capable young people who have become obsessed in their search for the "meaning of life" and as a result have gotten distracted and fallen by the wayside as they tried to move up the corporate ladder. Now, I'm not criticizing the search for meaning and purpose, because that's where you have to start if you hope to settle on a viable personal philosophy. But some people just can't make up their minds. They keep casting about, trying this or that set of values or experimenting first with one kind of personal satisfaction and then another. Today, it might be a different career focus. Tomorrow, it might be another sexual partner.

In contrast, if you have a firm personal philosophical foundation, you'll find you have one less thing—or one fewer set of things—to worry about. With the question of ultimate meaning and basic values settled, you can focus more of your efforts and attention on wrestling with business problems.

I should note again here, though, that I'm not advocating that you "get religious" or pragmatically affirm some world view just to make yourself more effective in your occupation. Obviously, the question of spiritual truth and commitment goes much deeper than productivity or satisfaction at work. But even so, it's important to understand that after you've reached a decision in this area of your life, you'll find you have a much better perspective on where your work should fit into your life as a whole.

• **A personal philosophy of life helps you establish standards of integrity.** Among the people I know at the top of the nation's major corporations, the personal quality that is regarded most highly is a solid, unwavering sense of integrity. The higher a person moves up in business, the more important it is for his peers and superiors to feel they can depend on his word. They have to know that he's a "straight shooter" in every sense of the word, one who won't cut moral corners to further his own interests.

These personal observations of mine also tend to be borne out by broader studies of the business community. The Korn/Ferry survey of senior managers found that after "concern for results," the most important trait that enhances executive success is "integrity." More than 66 percent of those questioned listed this quality as a key executive characteristic.

There are a number of very practical reasons why integrity is so important as you move up in the corporate hierarchy. For one thing, many business decisions are made quickly or have to be put in the hands of subordinates whose work can't always be double-checked. If you're going to weigh a person down with ever-increasing responsibilities, you have to be able to count on him, and that presupposes you trust and believe in him.

Honesty is one of the most important facets of personal integrity, because people want to be able to count on you when you research a problem and then present it to them for their evaluation and decision.

In one company I know, for example, a senior staff person named Jim was asked to research and test a certain product in a limited market and then report the results of that pilot test with his recommendations. Jim spent a great deal of the company's money to run the test, and the results were quite promising. But after he had completed the test and was going over his data, he discovered he had made an error in the way he had analyzed the results.

Panic gripped him. What should he do? He could admit to his error, be professionally embarrassed, and hope for the best. Or he could try what would in effect amount to a cover-up and hope that somehow the project would work out, despite his lack of basic honesty about the true outlook and meaning of his test.

Jim elected the cover-up route, and he proceeded to slant his preliminary report in such a way as to suggest that the prospects for his project were more promising than was actually the case. Soon, he found himself getting deeper and deeper into trouble. He suggested his superiors give him extra money to "fine-tune" the results he said he had gathered, and the company ended up spending almost twice as much as it should have.

Finally, it became clear that the preliminary report was inaccurate, and the blame was correctly attached to the dishonest staff person, Jim. As a result, any future he may have had at the company was effectively destroyed.

If Jim had just been honest at the outset, the chances are he would have saved his career and might even have earned a few points in the minds of some of his superiors because of his honesty. He might also have found that the error he thought was so bad could be compensated for in other ways. But his decision to dissemble led instead to his undoing.

In some ways, though, Jim's case is not typical of many people who are moving up in business. Outright, conscious dishonesty tends to be the exception rather than the rule. But a related character flaw which is more common is what I would call *intellectual dishonesty*, and I'd like to spend a little time now describing and illustrating this problem.

Both basic honesty and intellectual honesty are among the qualities I include under the general heading "integrity." But they differ from one another in that simple honesty involves being truthful and honest with others, while intellectual honesty involves being honest with yourself.

It's easy to deceive yourself about the true meaning of facts you've discovered in working on a company project if you have an overwhelming desire to see that project succeed. As you develop your reports and interpretations of your findings, you may not be consciously trying to concoct a dishonest scheme to pull the wool over your boss's eyes. But in becoming so obsessed with creating a "winner" you may begin to lie to yourself. That's the essence of intellectual dishonesty.

In my opinion, many people fail to live up to their potential because they're not willing to be honest with themselves. When a reasonable amount of research and thought reveals that a project is not going to work, they fail to "cut their losses" by walking away from that effort and moving on to something else. Instead, they say, "Let's study it some more. If we try just one more test, it may work."

In Jim's case, there seems to have been an element of

intellectual dishonesty, because he was hoping against hope that somehow the project would work out. He took the mistake one step further when he consciously doctored the representations and interpretations in his report. But the whole problem started because he had failed to be honest with himself and admit that the error in his analysis would eventually destroy the project he was trying to create.

Good judgment, which is the key quality in performing well as an upper-level executive, is rooted in the ability to be completely objective in making important business decisions. And objectivity arises directly from the capacity to assume an intellectually honest perspective on things, to step back and view a plan or project already in motion with cool detachment. But if a person's desire for a good result obscures the facts that he knows to be true, he becomes incapable of being objective or exercising good judgment. The last person you want to fool in business is yourself, but that's often the person you manage to fool first.

As I've already said, the inner moral fiber that it takes to be a person of integrity—and that includes intellectual honesty and a variety of other character traits—doesn't necessarily have to be rooted in traditional religious beliefs. I've known many men and women whose integrity I could count on implicitly even though they had never darkened a church or synagogue door.

But as you move higher up the corporate staircase, the stakes get bigger and the temptation increases to bend the rules a little to make yourself look better. And if you ever allow yourself to begin taking even the tiniest steps over moral lines, it gets easier each subsequent time to move further into dishonest territory.

Sometimes a relatively superficial personal philosophy of life may not be adequately grounded in broad, time-tested religious truths to provide a solid enough foundation to help you meet the moral challenges of the business world successfully. The only truly reliable means I've discovered to overcome the little temptations—and the big ones that inevitably follow—is to base my life on the moral authority of a historically tested religious faith, with all that such a commitment implies.

• **A strong world view can be an antidote to worry**. Every management level carries with it the necessity of making decisions—all sorts of decisions, large and small. And the more decisions you are confronted with, the more vulnerable you become to anxiety and worry.

When I first started out in business and began to move up in the hierarchy of store management, I discovered that it took me longer and longer to get to sleep at night. I had several personality characteristics that were working against me in this situation.

First of all, I'm a worrier by nature. My tendency is always to speculate about the outcome of any given project and wonder if I might have made some mistake that would affect the final result adversely. Also, I'm a perfectionist. I'm inclined to get concerned if something I'm doing isn't 100 percent right. But of course, *nothing* can ever be completely without fault. Finally, I have a very active imagination. Even if I haven't done anything wrong, my mind tends to wander to various circumstances over which I have no control. And I worry, "What if this boss does this, or that colleague does that—how would those actions affect my plans?"

I can still remember on several occasions being approached by a store manager at the end of a working day and being told, "Don, I'd like to see you first thing in the morning."

Then I'd go home, and my imagination—stimulated

by my natural tendencies to fret and be a perfectionist—would begin to work overtime. In bed on those nights, I'd run through an entire laundry list of reasons why my boss might want to see me—and, of course, all the items on that list would be bad. By the time I walked through his door the next morning I would be exhausted, because it would have taken me an hour or more to fall asleep. Also, I would be so agitated I'd practically have myself reprimanded before my boss opened his mouth.

In most of those situations, my boss's message would be something like this: "Don, you've been doing a good job, and I've decided to give you a raise."

After a few years of this nonsense, it finally dawned on me that perhaps my faith might have something to say about this anxiety problem. I recalled that passage in Matthew 6:34 where Jesus says, "Therefore do not worry about tomorrow, for tomorrow will worry about itself. Each day has enough trouble of its own" (New International Version).

That made sense, not just because it was a teaching rooted in my personal spiritual philosophy, but also because I realized worrying about things wasn't helping me one bit in resolving them. Most of the things you imagine are going to happen never come to pass. And even if they do, you've usually put yourself at a disadvantage in dealing with them if you've lost sleep the night before.

I finally realized I didn't have the time or energy to lie awake every night worrying about things I had no control over. So I decided to take the scriptural teachings at face value and refuse to worry! I just mentally wrapped up all my anxieties in a neat package, and I put them in God's hands, well outside my own mind every night. Now, I find I'm asleep within minutes after my head touches the pillow, and I'm in a much stronger position to wrestle with the *real* challenges that confront me each day.

Also, now that I'm in my present position, I'm finding that my control of even the *appearance* of anxiety has become especially important. This is particularly true with regard to the unspoken signals I may communicate to the other Penney employees.

I recall with some amusement a reaction to an incident that occurred during the 1974 recession. I heard that some of our people were quite worried that the company was in some sort of trouble because they had seen me with an extremely worried, sustained frown on my face a couple of days in a row on the elevator. Actually, as I thought back to those two days, I realized I hadn't been thinking about the company or the economy at all. On the first day I was upset because a new reed I had bought for my saxophone had split, and on the second day I was concerned about a decision we were having to make about a family vacation. I hate to think that some people may have lost sleep those nights because they were worried about what my frowns were indicating!

• **A comprehensive philosophy of life can turn you into a positive thinker.** If you can develop a positive, upbeat outlook on life and use this attitude as a basis to make yourself even more effective in dealing with co-workers, you'll almost certainly enhance your own productivity, as well as that of those who work for you. One likely result will be success in the majority of business projects you attempt. But if you're generally negative and fearful about life, you've lost before you even get started in wrestling with specific challenges on the job.

But it's not too easy to manufacture an optimistic attitude. If you don't genuinely feel it, the chances are you won't be able to pretend you do. So it's important that you actually *be* a positive sort of person. I find that a comprehensive value system is a good way to achieve this result.

In my own case, I find certain passages of the scriptures provide extremely helpful guidelines as I work to keep my own spirits up. For example, Proverbs 12:25 says, "Anxiety in a man's heart weighs him down, but a good word makes him glad" (Revised Standard Version). That "good word" may come from someone else, but it may also come from inside myself, as I try to be upbeat and enthusiastic in my conversations with others.

I need words like these when I return on Monday morning after a week or more away from the office and have to face mounds of paperwork rising a foot or more above my desk. It's easy to get rattled and become a negative thinker in such a situation: "How can I possibly do all this with the meetings facing me, and the trip to Washington later this week, and . . .?"

But then I try to shift gears and get into the positive-thinking and positive-talking frame of mind that will make me more productive. This procedure helps me tackle the job systematically, and the paperwork begins to melt away with a minimum of anxiety.

Of course, there are many variations on this theme of relying on your personal philosophy to find the silver linings on the clouds of your life. Some I might agree with, but others I find too unrealistic for the practical realities of the actual world.

I know one high-ranking executive who says, "The direction of our government and economy is in God's hands. So I don't get worried when the economic indicators take a turn for the worse. What's the point in worrying if things are ultimately out of your control?"

Now, I agree to some extent with this statement—but with at least one important qualification: I also think that human beings have to do everything they can to remedy bad situations in the government and in the business world. If an executive always projects a positive-thinking image to his workers, he certainly may influence them to think more the way he does. But if they learn that the reason for his optimism is purely a reliance on Providence, without some accompanying hard and effective work, they are likely to start feeling very uncomfortable.

I frequently pray that God will help me in my work, and I believe He answers those prayers. But I don't think He honors prayers that are offered up without a willingness on the part of the praying person to be an instrument in the answer to those prayers. In short, if you have a positive, mature value system and *use* it as a basis to make yourself even more productive, you'll most likely succeed in what you attempt. But if you're negative and fearful about life, you've lost before you even start.

• **Firm personal values enhance your ability to take criticism.** Some people can absorb critical comments about their work, improve their performance, and go right on as though nothing negative had happened. But others let criticism gnaw at them and may even find their career movement stymied if they hear a bad word.

For this second category of person, the problem may be that they have too fragile, uncertain a sense of self-confidence; or they may be so proud and sure of themselves that they are certain that no criticism of their work could possibly be valid. For those who have trouble taking criticism for these or other reasons, some sort of spiritual underpinning can be quite helpful in keeping a perspective on things.

I'm reminded of one young man I encountered a few years ago who was quite bright but for some reason made the assumption that he was always right and everybody else was always wrong. On one occasion, he gave a report before a group of senior officers, and one made a few comments about how he might improve his proposal.

"Yes sir, that sounds like a good idea," the young man responded in a cheery voice. And by all outward appearances he was maintaining a perfect equanimity in the face of the criticism.

But a few minutes later, he was overheard to say to one of his associates in the men's room, "That guy's suggestion was stupid. How did he ever get to where he is? I hope one day *we'll* be in a position to deal with incompetence like that!"

Actually, *this* fellow was the one who eventually got what was coming to him. On a number of other occasions, there was feedback that he couldn't take any slight correction of his work. Everything he touched became his pet brainchild, and he was visibly upset whenever anyone proposed a change in his work. The further up he moved, the more he verbally attacked those who criticized him. He soon reached his ceiling in the company, because his reputation had preceded him everywhere. Nobody wanted to work with him, and no officer wanted him on staff because it was common knowledge that he would become a troublemaker if there was any criticism of his performance.

In a case like this, the fellow would probably never know why he failed to move up higher in the company.

Even if someone told him he had a real problem accepting criticism, he would brush off the comment. He couldn't believe that the image he was projecting to others—an image of arrogance and total lack of humility and flexibility—could be having such a damaging impact on his career.

As for me, I don't like being told I'm wrong any more than anyone else does. In the first stages of my career, I had to rely by faith, rather than by experience, on verses like Proverbs 15:22: "Plans fail for lack of counsel, but with many advisers they succeed" (RSV).

But then as I moved up higher in the company and got more solid experience under my belt, I began to realize how true that piece of biblical advice is. You *have* to be a team player to succeed in business, and that means listening closely to suggestions and, yes, sometimes even to tough, untactful attacks on your work. Then the final step is to incorporate those changes that are valid. The result will usually be a better product and an additional number of supporters—those whose criticisms you've accepted—behind your project.

A comprehensive philosophy of life, then, is in every respect the "primary principle," or the basic foundation for a happy and successful business career. But it's dangerous ever to fall into the trap of assuming you've "got it made" or reached some sort of spiritual pinnacle. There is *always* a great deal of building that has to be done upon the foundation each of us has chosen.

Also, there's of course no guarantee that the person who develops a value system will succeed in material terms or be a winner by the world's standards. To achieve in those ways, it's necessary to go out and put in some hard, efficient work. As someone has said, God does provide food for the birds of the air, but He doesn't put the food in their nests. Or to put it in more contemporary terms, God may provide for all our needs, but He doesn't do it by mail.

If this sounds as though I'm advocating some sort of old-fashioned work ethic, that's exactly right, I am! Having a well-developed personal philosophy of life may give us access to inner strength and peace. But to translate those qualities into upward business mobility takes some intelligent planning and then a significant amount of mental and physical elbow grease to implement those plans.

Now, let's turn from the basic philosophical foundation that may undergird a successful career and take a closer look at how to plan and build the career itself. The first practical thing to do is to choose a specific business specialty and a specific company in which to pursue that specialty.

CHAPTER 4

The FIRST-STEP FACTOR:

Initial Career Choice and Choosing the Company That's Right for You

Some people get so worried about picking exactly the right job in exactly the right company at the outset of their careers that they become immobilized. They agonize, "If I make the wrong decision now, it's going to damage the development of my career and perhaps even my personal life."

This sort of anxiety is unnecessary, because it stems from a basic misunderstanding of how a person's career usually gets established in the real world. More often than not, careers *evolve*. They don't just appear full-blown and permanently immutable after an initial, momentous decision about what a person is going to do with the rest of his life.

So while it's true that a first career decision can be quite important, I also believe it's hardly ever irretrievably critical. No career decision is so important that you can't afford to decide you've made a mistake after a year or so and move into another field. And you'll usually be a much more purposeful and qualified person as a result of the experience.

All this leads me to the basic principle I call the *first-step factor*. Simply stated, this principle says your initial

career choice is important, and you should take plenty of time to research the field and think about your decision before you make it. But your first job need not be your last—and probably *won't* be your last!

Surveys have shown that top executives in this country work for an average of three companies during their careers. Also, those in senior management positions have worked an average of nineteen years for their final company, where they have made the greatest headway in moving up. What these figures say to me is that you do have to make up your mind early enough to give yourself enough time to rise toward the top levels of management. But it's by no means necessary to get discouraged and panicky if your first couple of jobs aren't quite what you hoped they would be.

If you look at my career, you might think it's advantageous for anyone who hopes to make it to the top to make the right career choice at the beginning. I've been with the JCPenney Company more than thirty years, since I was in my mid-twenties. Actually, though, JCPenney wasn't my first job. I had served in the U.S. Army for several years and got a good introduction to computer technology there. Then I had worked in several shoe stores, one of which competed with Penney's in Bradford, Pennsylvania. So up to the point that I joined Penney, I had quite a varied background.

Even if you shift around a little as a young person, as a general rule of thumb I would say it's important in most fields to make a firm career decision by the time you're in your middle to late twenties. Then, with the general direction of your working life set, you may also change jobs a few more times as you try to find the best niche in the field you've chosen.

But if you wait much longer than your late twenties to

settle on your basic career orientation, you'll be putting yourself at a disadvantage in your competition with other young people who have already made up their minds and have the jump on you by several years. The popular writer James Michener once said that he didn't think it was necessary to make up your mind about your life's work until the age of thirty-five. That may be fine for certain types of writing or other independent jobs. But in most traditional corporate careers, you're putting yourself at a disadvantage if you wait that long. For example, if you wait until age thirty-five to decide you want to be a marketing person or advertising writer, you'll likely be about ten years behind most of the people in the office.

I'm not highly attracted to people with résumés which reflect a hodgepodge collection of two years here in forestry, one year there in bartending, and two more years in another place as an apartment manager. On the other hand, for a person who has had some directed, purposeful movement early in his career, frequent job changes early on wouldn't bother me.

For example, I remember one résumé that indicated the applicant had spent the first few years working as a bookkeeper, and then had become a junior accountant for another company. Finally, he took a job as general auditor for another employer, got his C.P.A., and moved to another auditing department. His goal was to move up in financial management in a large company, and his job changes indicated he was on the right track.

Let me add one other word of qualification here: Although I believe there are many advantages to getting started early, I don't want to suggest that you shouldn't consider entering business as a career if you're thirty-five or forty. Many people that age and older—especially if they have a solid business education like an M.B.A.—can launch meaningful and successful careers. But there is almost always a limit to how far you can go if you wait until a relatively advanced age to get started. Those who make it to the top dozen positions in a large corporation or who end up running the company have usually gotten off to a relatively early start in their careers.

Still, there are nearly always exceptions to every rule. A few of those who enter the corporate world at a later age—but who have a certain "star" quality about their performance—may defy all I've said about starting early in developing a definite career pattern. But it's important to remember these people are the rare exceptions and to plan your own business goals accordingly.

So now, at whatever age you may be, you've definitely decided to take that first step into the world of business. What particular type of occupation should you concentrate on?

You may have prepared for a particular field in college and now need only to seek a company. You may have received some guidance from professional counselors at your college or university. For some people it takes more time, thought, and experience than are available in a school setting. If you haven't picked a definite field after your graduation, you may want to avail yourself of one of the many career-counseling services that abound in most of our cities.

If you feel you need some counseling, there are some general guidelines about what to look for. First of all, the price range for a battery of aptitude tests and counseling sessions runs from about $100 to $350 at the time of this writing. I would say that after you allow for inflation, any fees that run much above this range would be excessive, because most centers can give you all the help you need for less than $350.

A typical career-counseling center would have a staff of several professionals, including a number of licensed psychologists with Ph.D. degrees from recognized schools. Some organizations may base their fees on a rate per hour of about $50, but be sure that you know in advance how many hours it will take to get good advice at that rate. Otherwise, you may find yourself paying a much larger sum than necessary.

Even though many of the centers have highly trained professionals on the staff, they also frequently offer you a total of fifteen to twenty or more hours of testing and counseling in that limited $100 to $350 range. In other words, they are not billing you at the licensed psychologists' top rate for testing that can be done by lower-paid workers. So do some investigating and get some concrete estimates before you sign up with one of these services.

In addition to these independent testing centers, you might also want to consider companies that specialize in placing people in different jobs. On the lower levels in business, ordinary employment agencies can be of some help, because the better ones always keep extensive lists of job openings, many of which may not be advertised in your local newspaper. For a fee, these agencies may also help you put together a résumé and otherwise prepare yourself for job interviews. But as with the testing services, I would be careful about getting involved with a company that seems more interested in charging you exorbitant fees, primarily to "prepare" you for the job interview, than in concentrating on getting you the job itself.

There is also a related issue that I think is worth mentioning at this point, even though it concerns later career steps a person may take, rather than just the "first step" we're discussing in this chapter. On the higher levels of corporate management, there are employment services which I usually classify under two headings: (1) *executive placement firms*, which have as clients individuals who are looking for management positions; and (2) *"headhunting" firms*, which are hired by companies to go out and look for people who might fit into existing job openings.

Some of these services combine both the executive placement and the headhunting functions, and they vary greatly in expertise. So if a person in the middle management level or above is interested in going this route, it would be wise for him to look into several executive-search companies and ask each for referrals—people whom they have placed in different jobs in the past. Then the applicant might call a few of these people and ask their honest opinion about the quality of the firm's services. A little investigation along these lines should produce a good idea in a minimum amount of time about what each company can offer.

But now, let's return to the main topic under discussion—how to take that "first step" in launching a successful career in the practical business world. After you've decided on a *general* field, the next step is to pick a *particular* company.

With hundreds or perhaps thousands of potential employers out there in your chosen field, this step may seem confusing or even impossible. But as you already know, the first employer you choose may not be your last, so don't get overly concerned about making the perfect choice at the outset. You can't see into the future and know precisely what career pattern will develop from any given choice. But if you do proper research on certain types of companies and then make a reasoned choice, it's unlikely you'll go wrong!

Now as far as your own career is concerned, which

direction do you think you should take? In particular, should you choose a small or large company for your first job? The first logical step is to understand some things about large and small companies so that you'll be in a better position to decide which size would fit your own unique career objectives best.

Thinking big: One of the major advantages offered by many large corporations is that they may have better developed training programs for managers—and especially for management trainees—than smaller companies. There is a standing joke in some quarters of the business community that goes like this: One chief executive officer asks another, "Where do like to get your M.B.A.s from?"

"I like to get mine from Harvard and Wharton," his friend replies.

But a third who overhears the conversation pipes up, "I prefer to get mine from Procter & Gamble."

There are a number of big companies that have training programs which are as well regarded as Procter & Gamble's, and "graduates" of those courses are looked upon very favorably by other corporations. Because of the good reputations many large companies have for training their young workers well and giving them high-powered experience early in their careers, it tends to be easier to move from a big company to a small one than it is to go from small to big.

Another benefit offered by many larger companies is that there may be less likelihood of getting "blocked," or stuck in a particular position because all the positions above you are already filled by competent people. One reason for this is the obvious fact that there are more employees in a big company and, hence, a likelihood of more potential openings.

Another reason is that some big companies are known

for their flexibility in allowing workers to move from one specialty to a relatively unrelated area of operations. Lateral movements of this type are viewed as helpful in broadening the person's knowledge and practical experience.

For example, at IBM you might start off in a staff position, but your first promotion could be over to the "line" side of the business, such as one of the marketing offices. You might be switched back and forth this way to give you a better background in many areas of the company's operations—and the resulting breadth of background would prepare you better for an eventual position in upper-level general management.

A large corporation may also offer you a number of other attractive benefits, such as more insurance coverage and a better retirement program. And as you consider all these advantages, you may decide that there must be more security in a large corporation than a small one. But again, don't jump to any hasty conclusions.

Job security, you see, is a very complex issue that can't be understood solely in terms of the small-big comparison. It may be that there is less job turnover in large companies than in smaller ones—but that's not always the case. For one thing, it's important to distinguish between those companies, whether large or small, which *promote from within* and those which *hire from outside*.

Companies like IBM and JCPenney, which have extensive training programs for aspiring young managers and try to keep them throughout their careers, do relatively little hiring of outsiders. As a result, if you're admitted to one of these company training programs, do well in the courses, and then are conscientious in your work afterward, your chances of staying with the company throughout your working life are fairly good. You may not make it to the upper levels of management, but you can have a reasonable expectation that you won't lose your job or have your way blocked by the constant stream of new workers from the outside.

But other big companies look more favorably on job applications from employees in other companies—especially in the ranks of middle and senior management. In this type of job environment, your own position and your potential for upward mobililty may be less certain and secure than in those companies that promote from within.

One final word needs to be said about this issue of job security as it relates to the small company. Even though you may choose a small corporation that promotes from within and has a good track record of nurturing employees from the beginning to the end of their careers, there is a greater danger of losing your job through the acquisition of your company by a larger one. The acquiring company, by bringing in its own people or consolidating jobs, may push you and your particular area of responsibility right out of the picture.

We live in an era of mergers and acquisitions. So no matter how secure you think you are in your job, you almost have to be in one of the giant companies in our economy to be fairly certain that there's no danger of a corporate takeover.

Thinking small: Some people gravitate toward a smaller corporation almost instinctively. Perhaps they grew up in a small town and believe there will be more familiarity and intimacy in a company with fewer co-workers around. Or maybe they just like the idea of being a big fish in a little pond, and the small organization seems the best way to achieve this status.

But things aren't quite that simple. For one thing, a

worker may find himself in a small company where strained personal relationships are the rule rather than the exception—perhaps because the boss is a poor manager and his inadequacies have infected the majority of the small work force under him. Also, a person's hopes of becoming a big fish in a small company may quickly be snuffed out when he finds the few roads to the limited number of top positions blocked for one reason or another. For example, maybe those above him are doing a good job and have years to go before retirement.

So what are some of the facts about the advantages of a small company?

For one thing, if you choose the "think small" approach, you'll have more of an opportunity to be visible by top management from an early point in your career. If you make an excellent impression on those running the company, your chances of leapfrogging over your peers and moving to the upper echelons of the company will be much greater than in a big company, where promotions may occur in a more sequential way.

Another advantage of many small companies from the viewpoint of some people is that there may be fewer requirements for travel. Also, in a small corporation it may be less likely that you'll be transferred to an out-of-town branch—especially if there are no other branches in existence!

But any generalizations are dangerous, and it's important to evaluate your own needs first and then look closely at the *actual* situation in the company you're considering, whether it's large or small.

Some people also assume that big companies tend to stifle freewheeling business creativity and freedom of action and that small companies are much better suited for those with these tendencies. But once again, it's easy to generalize too broadly. There are various degrees in the need to be an independent operator, from the business "gunslinger" who has an irrepressible inner drive to start his own company to those with a milder need for creative entrepreneurial expressions.

The true gunslingers, who march to their own inner drummers and aren't influenced by the promise of rewards through steady upward movement in someone else's organization, don't belong in a corporate hierarchy. Even if they try extremely hard to fit in, they'll usually always feel out of place, and their ability to reach their full potential may well be stifled for good.

But the question for us is, are there ways to operate as an entrepreneur, at least to a limited degree, as an employee in companies that are already in existence? And if so, does the size of a company make any difference in terms of the number of entrepreneurial opportunities?

The answer to the first question is fairly easy: Yes, there are many ways you can operate as an entrepreneur as an employee in a corporation. Obviously, there are limits to how much freedom you have to be completely in control of implementing your own ideas and decisions. But often there's a great deal less restraint than you might imagine, especially as you move further up in the corporate hierarchy.

The answer to the second question is a little more difficult, because in general, the opportunity to be creative and exercise an entrepreneur-like control doesn't depend on whether you're in a small or large company. A small company may give you almost total freedom or may be so restrictive on your movements and decisions that you may think you're in prison rather than in business. And the same may be true of a big corporation.

So if it's important for you to have a fair amount of

freedom and to exercise an exceptional amount of control over projects assigned to you, you would do well to look closely at the traditions and practices of individual companies, rather than rely on any generalizations you may have heard about small or large companies.

After you've picked the size company that you feel will best suit your ambitions and personality, you're still left with the question "Which big (or small) company is best for me?"

You've already narrowed your choices down considerably, but you have to devote a little more time to serious thought and research before you can finally settle on the best specific organization. Take a look at your specialty—the kind of work that you're presently trained for or that you think you want to concentrate on for the next few years.

Suppose, for example, that you're quite good at mathematics and logical thinking and you're fascinated by computers. So you decide to be trained as a systems analyst. The most obvious companies for you to look into for job openings might be those like IBM or Control Data, which specialize in systems and data processing. But more often than not, what a person considers to be the "perfect" company for his skills and interests doesn't have a suitable job opening the first time he goes out looking for a position. So he finds he has to look at companies that he had relegated to his second, fifth, or tenth choices.

If this happens to you, as our hypothetical systems analyst—and it's likely it *will* happen on occasion to most people—it's important to keep your outlook on the job market broad and flexible enough to encompass those companies that have big, active systems and data-processing departments. And most major corporations these days would fall into this category. At JCPenney, for example, the usual way to move from the lower levels of the company to general management is to get involved in a "line" position like store management. But our systems department and related services are extensive enough to make these fields a solid foundation for upward career movement also.

My main point here is this: If you have to take a job with a company that is not your first choice or with one whose business operations seem to be quite different from your own special interests, you should definitely not be discouraged about your future prospects of becoming an upper-level executive. There is often plenty of opportunity for mobility within a company and upward movement to the general-management level, no matter what a person's specialized training.

There are some exceptions to this statement, of course. For example, a chemist in a quality-control lab of a large retailing chain probably will have relatively limited opportunities for promotion outside his specialty. It's likely, because of the nature of his job, that he'll only have a chance to impress his immediate supervisor with his skills. Those in other departments of the corporation probably won't have an opportunity to observe his work, and if they do, their lack of knowledge about what he does will prevent them from being able to evaluate him in any meaningful way.

But in most cases, if a person is good at what he does and demonstrates an above-average aptitude for management, he'll move up—perhaps to corporate levels well above his limited specialty. For example, a person with a background in computers, and especially systems analysis, should have a good chance to shine many places.

Why? For one thing, a good systems analyst will most likely be in close contact with managers in other departments of his company and will thus be in a position to be recognized by them for his good work. Also, by the very nature of his responsibilities, he should gain a fairly broad background in how different areas of the company operate and relate to one another.

But even though there may be many ways that it's *possible* to move to the highest levels in a given company, some routes are more promising than others. One way to ascertain some of the "smoother roads" to the top in a particular corporation is first to learn who the top six or so people are by checking a directory like Moody's or Standard & Poor's. Then thumb through *Who's Who* or other biographical listings to learn the previous training and backgrounds of these executives.

If you find that five out of six people are engineers and the sixth is a marketing expert—but you're an accountant—you may decide that your opportunities to move to the upper reaches of the corporate hierarchy are relatively restricted. Of course, it's true that the background for a chief executive officer at Penney probably won't be the same twenty years from now as mine is today. But I'm sure there will be some similarities—such as the heavy emphasis on store-management experience, marketing, and sales. So keep the backgrounds of the "in-house" achievers in mind when you're considering various companies.

In some related research, the Korn/Ferry survey of top executives found that of the more than 1,700 executives questioned, a large majority, 78 percent, began their climb to the top in one of three major specialties: marketing/sales, finance/accounting, and professional/ technical work, such as law or engineering. Many have moved beyond their original backgrounds into general management. But they have found these three areas particularly useful as a springboard to bigger things.

Before we pursue this line of discussion any further, however, I should inject one note of caution: You've undoubtedly read some press reports about various wunderkinder in their late thirties or early forties who rise to the upper echelons in business. But I don't believe that for most upper-level executives there is any such thing as a "fast track" to the top. It's my impression that it usually takes time, patience, and persistence to rise to the senior management levels in most companies, and some recent studies on this subject tend to bear me out.

For example, a 1980 Arthur Young & Company survey of chief executive officers in the biggest American companies found that the typical chief executive was fifty-nine years old and had been in his present job for at least seven years. This means that these men—and the respondents were all men except Katharine Graham, chairman of the Washington Post Company—reached the top of their companies *after* they were fifty years old. Also, the chief executives in this survey had been with their organizations for an average of twenty-four years, and more than 35 percent had had only one employer.

So for most people who have their sights set on a position in senior management in a large company, it is wise to think in terms of steady but gradual progress upward. Your first job may not be your last; but at the same time it's important at some point early in your career to decide you're going to settle in for the long haul in a particular company. That's the only way you'll be able to build up the kind of experience and personal relationships you'll need to reach your full potential in business.

Now, here's one final bit of advice if you are in the

early stages of your career and are still trying to find that special company that you can feel comfortable with for a significant number of years: *Use a "shotgun" approach to job-hunting!*

You can't necessarily expect the first or second or even the tenth firm you contact to give you exactly the job you want—or, for that matter, any job at all! So be prepared to send out dozens of résumés and go to an equal number of interviews. That way, you'll be less likely to become discouraged if you're rejected at several places, and you'll also increase the odds of landing the best possible job you can find.

I've seen scores of great résumés from great job candidates. But we've had to turn many of them down simply because the timing was wrong. At any point, we might not have needed anyone in the particular area in which the individual was applying. But then a couple of months later, just the right opening for that person we turned down might show up. When you use a shotgun approach to job-hunting, you'll greatly increase your chances of hitting that one company that is looking for a person just like you, at the very moment you're searching for such a job yourself.

After you've found a job and company that seem right for you, you may still decide after a few years, "I don't think I'm going anywhere in this place. It's time to move on!"

Sometimes your instinct to try another company may be just the right thing for you to do—despite those statistics that we just cited about how the typical CEO stays in one company for such a long time. Statistics and averages can take you only so far in planning a career. Ultimately, everybody has to rely finally on what he feels are the best uses of his individual interests and talents. And this means finding a specific company and job which will afford the greatest freedom to develop individual abilities, from the lowest to the highest rungs of the corporate ladder.

But it may also be that you're 180 degrees wrong in feeling it's time to move to another company. You may be completely misreading the plans that management has for you and as a result miss out on a tremendous opportunity—one which almost certainly would have been yours if you'd only waited patiently a few more months, or perhaps another year or so.

But how can you tell? How can you evaluate your potential in a company when you're on the bottom side looking up? Let's move on now to a consideration of these questions and others that concern how you can develop your own personal career plan.

CHAPTER 5

DEVELOPING *a* PERSONAL CAREER PLAN

No one, to my knowledge, has ever developed a complete personal career plan overnight.

It takes time, patience, and a considerable amount of experimentation to settle on the precise direction that one's working life should take. This is not to say, of course, that a person can't settle on a definite occupational goal at an early point, work toward it, and even eventually achieve it. But the exact path that the individual treads to that ultimate goal often becomes clear only over a rather long period of time.

In some ways, developing into an upper-level executive is a lot like developing into a topflight professional athlete. If you read the sports pages occasionally, it may sometimes seem that certain star athletes burst onto the scene out of nowhere. But actually, a closer study of their background and training *always* shows years of preparation and hard work.

All of the best pro sports figures have more natural ability than average. But to get where they are, they have often had to begin intensive training at a young age and fine-tune their evolving skills at progressively more challenging plateaus of competition. As they work to enhance their special strengths on the playing fields, they must also try hard to shore up their weaknesses. During this training, they may well suffer setbacks and failures in the effort to achieve an overall improvement in their abilities. And it's necessary for them constantly to reevaluate the ways they are attempting to better their performance and move to greater heights in their sport.

A business career pattern develops in much the same way. An upper-level executive doesn't just appear in his job out of nowhere. He's usually been in his field—and often in the same company—for decades. More often than not, he's taken more time to study his trade and learn management skills than have the large majority of his contemporaries. And even though he may have formulated certain general, long-range career goals, he remains flexible about the exact route he'll take to reach them.

Sometimes, the upwardly mobile manager may seem to be making no forward progress while others, who appear to be inferior to him in ability, move ahead. On other occasions, he may move rapidly from one promotion and raise to the next so that his peers look as though they are standing still in his wake.

Over time, you should learn to be patient, but not complacent. You may well sense intuitively when you've reached a real roadblock to your ambitions, and when you're merely encountering an obstacle which, after you clear it, will teach you something about yourself that will make you stronger executive material than ever.

One practical and extremely important consequence of this patient and flexible approach to career development is that it should put you in a better position to sense more accurately whether to stick with your present job—despite delays or setbacks in your upward progress—or move on to another company. You may be asking, "Have I overstayed my welcome in this present company, or should I hold on for a while because of the promise of better times to come?'' To answer this question—and others related to your overall personal career plan—here are six principles, based on observations and experience, which I feel can serve as helpful guidelines.

1. Develop a limited concept of success.

On its face, this point may seem counterproductive to your ambitions. After all, aren't you supposed to shoot for the stars if you hope to get to the top?

I agree completely that a successful person is one who always must be ready to climb that next mountain. But if you keep your eyes on the *top* of the mountain rather than on the trail right in front of you, you may get lost and never realize your ultimate goal. Keep your ambitions focused on the job at hand—that's the only way to do superior work and put yourself in a position so that you'll have the best chance of moving up to the next level.

Actually, I stumbled onto this principle accidentally. When I first started working at the JCPenney Company, I was hired as a shoe salesman. I had been selling shoes off and on since I was fifteen years old in various stores, and I enjoyed the experience of meeting the public in this kind of work.

My only goal when Penney hired me was that one day I wanted to run the biggest shoe department in the company. Today, this would be a fairly ambitious goal, because our biggest shoe department is larger than several of our smaller stores put together. But when I got started with the Penney Company, that wasn't the case. I knew something about selling shoes, and I figured it was reasonable to assume I could learn a few management skills and have a good chance to realize this goal. That was the extent of my ambition at the time, and I'm glad that my fantasies of success didn't reach beyond that level.

Of course, it would be an oversimplification to say that anybody who thinks beyond his present job is going to fail to fulfill his long-range ambitions, because that just isn't true. Some people with big hopes for themselves *do* succeed in realizing their expectations.

The real problem arises when these ambitions begin to *preoccupy* the employee to the extent that he never feels satisfied with his present position and can't concentrate fully on the job at hand. This type of person, no matter how much natural ability he possesses, tends to be one of the top two or three who is always considered for promotion—but also in most cases he tends to be the runner-up, the one who lacks that extra edge that will keep him moving toward the upper management levels.

But without attempting to dissect the psyche of any of these individuals, I've concluded that their problem often goes back to an overactive imagination that focuses too much on a *distant* concept of success. In contrast, the person who succeeds in reality, and not just in his mind, tends to be a practical activist who throws himself wholeheartedly into the tasks at hand and achieves a more *immediate* series of successes by "getting his hands dirty" through hard work.

In other words, it's fine to shoot high in your company—in fact, it's essential to have long-range goals if you hope to keep the overall movement of your career on track. But it's also important to guard against excessive global fantasies, because they may dilute your ability to put 100 percent into the job at hand. And your current job is the key to future promotions, because it's important to be the best, or close to it, at *each* position you hold if you hope to keep moving up.

There's also another rather helpful way of looking at

this matter of ambition and success fantasies. I discovered over the years that if I kept my attention focused on my present job, *realistic* ideas for advancement to the next rung on the corporate ladder began to appear from the actual work I was doing.

For example, as I sold shoes in that first Penney store, I had a chance to observe managers at different levels, and I became aware that I might be able to move up into their jobs one day. I knew I could run a good shoe department and felt I could compete with anybody on that level. But I hadn't thought about trying the men's clothing department or women's lingerie. So I spoke to the store manager about my desire to move up and asked him to keep me in mind for one of those positions in the future.

My movement up in the Penney Company began just this way. I never looked beyond the next step—at least almost never. *Occasionally* in my career I have fantasized about much higher positions in the company. But most of the time I've maintained a kind of "tunnel vision," with my attention focused only on the work in front of me. And I'm convinced that this approach works best for most people who hope to move up into senior management.

I've also known people who formulated what they considered to be ideal timetables for their progress in a company. They might set their sights to be a district supervisor by age thirty-five, or whatever. The problem is that if they didn't reach that goal by the predetermined age, they were opening themselves up for tremendous disappointments and a potential loss of perspective on their careers.

The irony is that if you tell yourself, "I must reach district supervisor by age thirty-five," and then give up when you fail to meet that goal, you may be committing a kind of "occupational suicide" just before your most productive and successful years arrive. For example, it may be that you would have become a district supervisor by age thirty-seven and then have shot ahead at double-time through the next few levels of management. Your career timetable is a very personal thing, and the only way you can move at your best personal rate is to concentrate on the task at hand and do a superior job.

So once again we return to a major theme I keep emphasizing in this book: If you work hard and do a good job, it's almost inevitable that management will recognize your abilities and promote you.

Why? In the first place, there's a practical, dollars-and-cents reason for your boss to notice the job you're doing: It's in his interests to identify the best people and put them in the most responsible jobs. In this way, the company will be most likely to generate profits—and thereby enhance your boss's reputation as a good manager. A corollary to this principle, by the way, is that office politics and Machiavellian power plays are far *less* important than your own productivity as a key to advancement and the ultimate realization of your ambitions.

Having a limited concept of success, then, is not at all in conflict with being ambitious. Rather, it can help you direct your ambition into the most fruitful channels. Healthy ambition in business should always cause the individual to focus on being the best. Then the question becomes, the best at what? The answer: the best at what you're presently doing.

2. Expect a bad boss.

We hear a lot these days about the advantages of positive thinking, and I agree that an ability to look on the bright side of a bad situation can be a tremendous asset in helping you get through hard times. But to succeed in business, it's also necessary to avoid unrealistic optimism and anticipate the bad along with the good. Otherwise, when something unpleasant does happen, you may find yourself being caught unprepared.

One particularly important kind of negative thinking for you to engage in is to expect an occasional bad boss. And take it from me, it's quite likely you'll eventually encounter a supervisor who will make you want to pack your bags and look for work elsewhere.

I've been fairly lucky during my career, because most of the people I've worked for were fair and easy to get along with. But I did run into one supervisor early in my career who almost caused me to leave the Penney Company. I was working in a Penney store at the time, and this fellow, who was one level above me, was given to screaming periodically at his employees.

I recall one time I had displayed some merchandise in a way that I thought would be especially attractive to my customers. But he walked in and shouted, "How can you be so stupid to have those things lined up that way, Seibert? Where were you when they passed the brains out? You're never going to make it in this business!"

Several of my sales associates were within hearing during this outburst, and I felt embarrassed and humiliated at being demeaned in front of my staff this way. An impulse welled up in me to shout an insult back at him, but something told me not to respond in kind— at least not in public. I sensed that if I started yelling, I'd do myself far more harm than good, and so I kept my mouth shut.

But when a similar incident occurred again, I decided I had to do something about it, so I arranged to see this supervisor in private. Our conversation went nowhere, because he was completely oblivious to the impact he was having, and I couldn't seem to get the message across that I was unhappy with the way he was treating me.

Unfortunately, the abuse didn't end with the shouting, and I wasn't by any means the only victim. This man was often insensitive to the personal and family needs of his employees, and a number of people actually resigned because of the abuse. In the face of this unpleasantness, I began to wonder, "Is it really worth it for me to hang around this place? Surely other companies have better working conditions than this!"

I shared my concern with a colleague in another department of the store, and he revealed he had been running into similar problems with this same supervisor. "But I'm not about to let this guy drive me out of the company!" he said. "I haven't found a guy yet who's mean enough to run me off. I've decided to develop a thick skin for people like that, because I know I can manage a Penney store—and I'm going to do it someday."

Actually, he eventually *did* become a store manager, and his determination under adverse conditions was just what I needed to hear. He made me want to dig in and weather the present storm because there was the promise of better times ahead. As I looked around at the other managers in that store, I began to gain a better perspective on my own situation. This bad boss I had been unlucky enough to draw was an exception. In fact, he was the only bad supervisor in the entire group.

Also, even if I wasn't having such a good time working under this man, it dawned on me that I still had something to learn from him. Granted, the lessons were often negative, but I could see that this fellow was a great case study in how *not* to treat employees if you wanted to get the best performance out of them.

Here are just a few of the lessons I took to heart: I saw how demoralizing it is to be criticized by your boss in front of customers and other employees. I also realized how important it is always to think before you comment on the performance of subordinates. Finally, I knew firsthand how unhappy you can make an employee by failing to treat him and his family and personal problems fairly.

I'm sure that the stressful experience of working under that man actually helped make me a better manager, because I developed a strong need not to make the same mistakes he had. These bad experiences, as well as the good ones, can be instrumental in shaping you into a more effective executive if you can just learn to stand back, assume an air of detachment, and allow yourself to be instructed by *everything*, both negative and positive, that happens to you.

One of the best images of this process of practical learning that comes to my mind is a short IBM film I viewed many years ago. The purpose of the film was to describe part of the mechanism of computers, but I drew a much broader lesson from the presentation. The film clip showed two South Sea Islanders walking along in a jungle, with little balloons over their heads that showed what they were thinking.

First of all, they saw a coconut fall from a tree and break in half, and one of the halves dropped into a stream and started floating along in the current. Then they noticed some tall palm trees blowing in the breeze and also some leaves from other trees floating down to the ground in the wind.

With these observations tucked away in their minds, the two natives came to the shore of the island, and as they walked along the sand, they looked over the water and saw another island in the distance. Both wished they could get over to that other island, but they knew they couldn't swim that far.

Then the information they had stored up began to come back to them: They saw a large version of the coconut shell, with a tree that became a mast and a leaf that became, in their minds' eyes, a sail. In other words, they converted their observations into a primitive sailboat that finally enabled them to travel across to the other island.

This little vignette shows not only how a computer works, but also the process by which our minds store up information which can later become productive ideas. And I suppose, by taking the analogy one step further, you could include *negative* observations and experiences as well as positive ones as part of the example. In other words, these two fellows might have seen that a broken, defective coconut shell wouldn't have stayed afloat, or a weak branch or palm tree wouldn't have made an adequate mast.

So when you find yourself embroiled in a bad situation with some insensitive boss, try to get into the habit of behaving as an outside observer might. Try to conduct yourself in a way that minimizes the disruptions and tensions caused by the bad supervisor. And above all, watch this person closely and learn from him, so that you can avoid the same mistakes when you move into a similar position. With this kind of attitude, you'll become a better executive yourself, and you'll be much less likely to allow one bad boss to drive you out of the company.

3. Don't look for ultimate meaning in life on the job.

One of the mistakes I find businesspeople making is that they expect, consciously or subconsciously, to find total fulfillment for their life in their work. In a way, I suppose it's natural to have such expectations, because those of us who work full-time spend most of our waking hours on the job. As a result, it may seem logical to think, "If I spend so much time on my career, then I have a right to expect most of the satisfaction in life will come from that career."

Unfortunately, though, a job rarely provides that kind of total fulfillment. I recall one young woman who started off as a good secretary but found that wasn't providing her with the challenge she wanted. So she earned an M.B.A. and got a job as an account executive in a top advertising firm.

She began to work long hours in an effort to move up in her company, and she did get some attractive promotions and raises. But still, she wasn't really happy. And the large amount of time and mental energy she was putting into her job made her neglect her husband and family. A divorce was the eventual result, and now, although she's successful by society's standards, she is also profoundly unhappy.

This young woman was in effect on a *spiritual* quest, but she was looking in the wrong place. It may sound strange for the chief executive officer of a large corporation to be saying this, but I want to make sure you get the point: A career in business can provide you with a great deal of satisfaction, excitement, and material and emotional rewards. But don't expect *any* job, in management or elsewhere, to be a substitute for ultimate meaning in life. If you do have such expectations, you're sure to be disappointed.

As you can see, this discussion is bringing us back to the "primary principle" we examined in some detail earlier in this book. If you first come to some definite conclusions about your own personal value system, then you'll be in a much better position to enjoy your work. But if you try to make your work serve as a substitute for those deeper foundations, you could be heading for disappointment and unhappiness.

4. Filter company gossip.

Every company has the equivalent of what people in the military call the "guardhouse lawyer." This individual has usually been around the corporation for a while and has the ability to assimilate bits and pieces of information and various rumors. He then disseminates them in the form of authoritative, coherent opinions about how company politics works and makes seemingly plausible predictions about the future prospects of individual employees.

The problem is that this self-appointed expert is usually wrong more times than he's right. And if you rely on him too heavily for advice, you'll find yourself making unwise decisions that could even affect the direction of your career.

One young woman came in to talk to me about a fear she had that she was caught in a dead-end job. "Four people who had this job before me all say it's a dead end, and I want something more than that out of my career," she complained.

But as I probed the sources of her information, I

learned that the four people she was citing as authorities had been with the company less than two years! One of them in particular had already acquired a reputation as a guardhouse lawyer, so the young woman sitting in my office was suffering from the consequences of several sources of unreliable information.

"I'm glad you came to me to discuss this, because it's really unwise to rely on people who try to do an informal analysis of your career in the company cafeteria," I said. "In the first place, those you've been talking to haven't been around the company long enough to know what the future holds for them—much less for you. They may *think* that job is a dead end, but I can point to many people who have used the position you hold right now as a springboard for much better things. As a matter of fact, a couple of them are now in profit-sharing positions."

She left our discussion with a somewhat better perspective on her situation than when she had entered my office. But I found myself wondering how many other employees in large corporations have been misled because they haven't taken the time to check out the "facts" they have picked up in washroom conversations.

It's tempting—and quite natural—to listen to company gossip. But it's important to be objective about everything you hear, at least to the extent that you *can* be objective. Much of the loose talk you hear will probably be negative rather than uplifting, and an excessive amount of badmouthing directed toward supervisors, promotion opportunities, or any other aspect of your company may threaten to damage your overall morale.

For one thing, you may begin to feel the situation is so bad in your company that there's really no point in even attempting to advance yourself. At the other extreme, you may hear rumors to the effect that there are so many super workers around that you could never measure up to their performance.

For example, there are the stories in every company of the "living legend"—the hotshot who came along a few years or months ago and whose career is soaring so high that he's set a standard that no ordinary person could possibly follow. Again, discussion of this superstar usually occurs in the lunchroom, and as you listen to tales of his exploits, you gradually decide, "What chance do I have to follow a person like that?"

Although I was never seriously affected by specific "living legend" stories, I do recall a related problem I had early in my career. I sat down one evening when I was in a middle management position in one Penney store and tried to figure the mathematical possibility of my becoming a senior manager. When I calculated the number of employees at my level in the company and the much smaller number of higher positions, the odds against me seemed astronomical.

What I failed to understand during that depressing mathematical exercise was, first of all, that a superior effort on the part of any individual will always be recognized. That means if you turn in a standout performance, the odds in your favor will greatly improve. Second, I didn't understand how the internal "promotion mathematics" works in a large corporation. No matter how many people may *seem* to be standing in the way of your upward movement, the field of competitors always thins out dramatically through job transfers, resignations, retirement, and promotions to higher levels of management.

So my advice to you would be this: Learn to filter out what you can use in the informal information network in your company, and be careful to identify and discard what is just misinformation. Also, don't be afraid to consult your boss about some of the things you hear—or the theories you've concocted on your own, like my "promotion mathematics" scheme. If he's at all sensitive to the people under him and the environment in which they work, he'll be able to put some of the rumors and popular theories into a broader, more accurate framework.

Remember: You are a unique individual with special qualities that can help you rise above the seeming mathematical odds against you, and also help you become one of the exceptions to the common "wisdom" (or, more often, folly) of company scuttlebutt.

5. Take a deep breath before you walk out.

This is one of the hardest pieces of advice I can give, because what I'm suggesting is that you consider hanging in there in your present job, *even if you lose out on a promotion to one of your peers*.

The main reason I take this approach is that I believe it's highly likely, no matter what company you work for, that your superiors have *some* sort of plan in mind as they move people under them into various positions. Their plan may be far from perfect, and they may make mistakes in awarding a particular promotion to one person and not to another. But in most cases, a high level of performance and a good work attitude will eventually be recognized and rewarded. So even though your bosses may promote somebody else first, you may still move into an even more attractive job a little later—if you'll just be a little patient.

On occasion during my career I've found myself in a "holding pattern" while someone else moved ahead of me, into a more responsible, higher-paying position. Sometimes I worried briefly about the meaning of these moves. But I found that I could get rid of any anxiety by taking two steps:

First of all, I would raise the issue of the promotion with my boss and ask him, in a tactful way, if there was some reason why I hadn't been tapped for the position. (On at least one occasion, a supervisor took me aside and explained the meaning of the promotion before I had a chance to bring the subject up myself.)

Second, after getting some information on the meaning of the other person's promotion, I ascertained as well as I could whether there was any indication that I had reached some sort of ceiling in my own upward movement in the company. Then, when I determined there wasn't any such indication, I pushed all thoughts of the incident out of my mind and focused my attention once more on doing my best job on the tasks at hand.

If you initiate any conversation with your boss about the meaning of another worker's promotion, it's important to do it in a positive, upbeat way. This is not the time to challenge your boss on what led him to his conclusion.

But it may be appropriate for you to express a concern about your own career and to stress your desire to increase your own level of responsibility. You may also want to comment generally on the promotion that was announced. For example, you might say something like "I hope I'm in the running for something like that. If there's anything I need to do to improve my own performance, I hope you'll tell me."

But suppose you find yourself passed over a second or third time? At what point should you start reevaluating your future in the company?

I believe that it's often dangerous to think of leaving a company the first time you lose out on a promotion. But it's hard to generalize about this subject, because each person's situation is different. If you're a relatively young person, you may be making a serious mistake by leaving in a huff when you're passed over once for a position—particularly if you have met with your supervisor, expressed your concern, and received some positive feedback. If you'll just exercise a little patience, you may well find that your boss has something much more attractive in store for you in the near future.

On the other hand, if you're in your fifties and have been passed over for the last key job you think you're qualified to hold in your company, that's when the time may have arrived to review your options, including making yourself available to other organizations. If you wait for the next opportunity to be promoted, you may find it's too late, both in your own company and elsewhere. It is also quite possible that your present position, with its accumulated retirement benefits and other advantages, will still be more attractive than anything outside your company, anyway.

So to summarize, there are three things you should do as you take that deep breath when someone else has been promoted instead of you: (1) Through a face-to-face discussion, determine as best you can exactly how you stand with your boss—whether he seems, on the whole, positive, negative, or merely neutral. (2) During that discussion, recognize that your boss can't reveal everything about his future plans to you, so you'll have to accept some vagueness in his answers. (3) Finally, make a realistic evaluation of your present situation to determine whether there really are possibilities for you if you stay on.

If you come up with a positive response to each of these points, then be *patient* and wait for that next promotion opportunity to appear. You may be pleasantly surprised, and even inclined to agree with the eighteenth-century poet Nathaniel Cotton, who wrote:

> *To be resign'd when ills betide,*
> *Patient when favours are deni'd,*
> *And pleas'd with favours given—*
> *Dear Chloe, this is wisdom's part;*
> *This is that incense of the heart*
> *Whose fragrance smells to heaven.*

6. Learn how to work for another person.

You'd be amazed how many people—especially if they are very bright—find it difficult to work for others. You may even have this problem yourself, but up to this point you may not have identified it for what it is.

If a person has succeeded in everything he's done—had a 4.0 average in school, was president of the student body, and generally has established himself as a high achiever—he may well have great difficulty working for someone who is (or who he thinks is) his intellectual inferior.

But if you're in a junior position, it's dangerous to jump to any conclusions about how much more you know than your boss. It may well be that you have a greater command of the facts involved in any given situation. But he's been with the company longer and may well have developed a "feel" or a sense of judgment for different issues that you haven't yet acquired.

In this regard, I'm reminded of a conversation I had with a district manager who was over me a number of years ago. He asked me to do something, and I thought he was wrong and told him so.

"You may well be right, Don," he replied. "But I think if we look at our track records at this point—if we compare our successes and failures—you'll find that I'm right about 70 percent of the time and wrong about 30 percent of the time. Until you think you can be right more than 70 percent of the time, we'll do it my way."

He was saying that the odds were in his favor because he had a broader experience in the business than I did. I might well be right on a particular issue. But my boss had a longer proven track record than I did. He had what is often called in business slang "hands-on work experience," while all I had at that point on many subjects was just theoretical knowledge. And it's the hand's-on experience that most often gives you the sense of perspective and judgment that's necessary to make important management decisions.

So even if you're a bright person and you're certain you know more about the science of business management than your boss will ever know, don't automatically write him off as a hindrance or, at best, a neutral presence. If you do, he'll likely write you off as well, and you'll certainly be opening the way for him to become an obstacle to your upward movement. Moreover, you may well be missing out on an important and easily tapped source of practical wisdom—wisdom that you'll still have to acquire later. But you'll have to do it without his help, and possibly through a relatively painful process of trial and error.

As you can see, these six guidelines for developing your personal career plan are designed to make you think long and hard before you decide to pick up your marbles and shift your career game to another company. I get rather concerned sometimes at the impatience and cavalier attitudes that some people display toward their jobs. The slightest little frustration may be enough to make them give up and start looking for another position.

But that simply doesn't make sense! No boss or job or corporation is perfect, and you're being unrealistic and completely unfair to your own chances for success if you assume any sort of perfection.

So before you decide to leave your present position, do some careful analysis of the reasons why you're moving and the advantages and strengths of making a move. Sit down with a pad of paper, and on one sheet list all the things you have to lose by moving. A few points that may come immediately to mind are your knowledge of your company and its business, retirement benefits, other fringe benefits like vacation time, the seniority you've acquired, and the goodwill you've built up in your present job.

Then, take another sheet of paper and write down the advantages of leaving. Perhaps you've been passed over for promotion too many times. Or you've been offered another job that pays much more and appears to put you on a faster upward track in another comparable corporation.

When you've completed these two lists, take a third sheet of paper and summarize your findings in a sort of "Career Balance Sheet." Do the benefits of moving outweigh the detriments? Or are you really better off staying in your present job a little longer?

You may decide that your present position is inferior to one you've been offered. But perhaps you're getting along in years, and the risk of losing part or all of your retirement credits outweighs all other considerations. The only way to evaluate this issue and any others that may arise is to see all the factors in front of you, in black and white. Then you'll be in a position to make an intelligent decision about whether to stay with your company or start looking for another job.

Your career plan, then, is a highly personal thing, with a movement and a pace that reflects your special interests and abilities, and no one else's. The question "Should I stay with this company?" is one that only you can answer. Also, the precise turns, detours, and shortcuts that constitute your movement inside a company are often more within your control than you may realize at first glance.

But perhaps most important of all, it is within your power to step back every so often and try to evaluate exactly where your career is headed, and whether or not you like that direction. There are frequently certain weaknesses in junior managers which, if corrected, can open the door to much faster advancement. Furthermore, many weaknesses, such as the ones discussed in this chapter, *can* be corrected—but the person must first take an honest look at himself and then set his mind to making some improvements.

So start moving right now toward understanding yourself better, with *all* your strengths and weaknesses. Armed with that knowledge, you're ready to begin to develop your own special career plan which can give you a solid foundation for climbing to higher levels in your company.

CHAPTER 6

HOW *to* SUCCEED
THROUGH CREATIVE
RISK-TAKING

Many people assume there is little or no room for creativity in an established corporation, and especially not in a *big* corporation. In this view, there *may* be a place in business for the great freewheeling thinkers, artistic temperaments, mavericks, and rebels—but only in highly individualistic, entrepreneurial ventures, far outside the staid corporate world.

But I would beg to differ. Every great creative expression, in whatever field of endeavor, must occur within a certain structure, a certain set of rules, if you will. The architect can try new ways of shaping form and space; but in the last analysis, he must follow certain engineering principles if he expects his building to be safe and continue to stand over the years. The writer can experiment with various styles and combinations of words; but he is still bound to using a certain known language which will be printed and distributed in a standard fashion, if he hopes to communicate with his readers. Even the fine artist has to operate within the general framework of certain tools, traditions, and trends.

Much the same set of principles applies in big business. If you hope to move to the upper levels of your company, you have to operate within a certain framework of policies and strategies that have been established over the years by top management. But there is still plenty of room to maneuver within the limits of the system through an approach that I call "creative risk-taking."

In explaining this concept, I find it's helpful to distinguish between (1) a company's set policies, strategies, and tactics, and (2) the implementation of those policies.

Company policies may include written rules of conduct, such as "No company employee shall accept a gift from any company supplier and any acceptance of such a gift shall be grounds for immediate dismissal." Another kind of policy would be a rule that a company's stores must never sell "second-quality merchandise"—or irregular items with various flaws.

Strategies and tactics, on the other hand, focus more on setting the company approach for operating in the marketplace. Guidelines for current company advertising, for example, may fall in this category.

The wise employee who has his eye on higher positions will be careful to conform to company policies, strategies, and tactics—just as the wise architect will obey basic engineering principles and governmental building codes. If you try to get "creative" and show yourself to be a maverick or rebel on the policy, strategy, or tactics level, you may well be heading for big trouble and even the loss of your job.

So remember: You can challenge a policy and perhaps get it changed by going through proper company channels and procedures. But if you just ignore it, you do so at your peril!

On the level of *implementation* of policy or strategy— where guidelines for action and conduct haven't been as clearly spelled out by top management—there is much more room to be creative. In fact, if you want to succeed in a big way in business, it's absolutely necessary to give your mental processes and creativity free rein in this area—and even take a few personal risks when you happen upon a good idea that requires some aggressive advocacy. The person who subordinates all his creativity and plods along, playing it completely safe and going only by the book in his work, won't go very far.

For example, in an economy in which there is a concern about energy and its costs, it's a policy in many companies to be as energy-efficient as possible. Big corporations are spending a lot of money and time researching ways to conserve energy in company offices, stores, and factories.

In the Penney Company, we have formulated many guidelines for stores to conserve more energy. But there are still stores where an operations manager has come up with a new idea to reduce energy consumption even further and has gone ahead, on his own, to put that idea into effect.

No company can continue to exist without implementing new ideas that enhance profit-making and cost-cutting in the rapidly changing marketplace. Honest profits are the ultimate goal of any corporation, and this means you have to have people in the corporation who are capable of coming up with new money-making concepts. Usually, the people with the best ideas—or at least an openness to implementing those ideas—are going to rise to the top levels in any company.

In other words, if you hope to do well in your organization, you should cultivate your own entrepreneurial instincts. In this chapter I want to show you a few of the many ways you can go about cultivating your business creativity.

But first, let me mention one important distinction:

Unlike the freewheeling entrepreneurs who go out and start their own businesses from the ground up, you have to *fit into an already existing team* if you go to work for a corporation. As a result—as we've already seen in our discussion of the importance of recognizing company policies—your entrepreneurial instincts have to be expressed in a disciplined way. You can't have a thousand people running around in a thousand different directions in a large company and still hope to get to your final destination—a coordinated effort that results in a maximum return in profits.

But with this word of caution in mind, you should get into the habit of looking for opportunities that may entail some personal risk. If you're quite confident you've found one, then the time may be ripe for you to be innovative.

You should keep one hard fact in mind, however: If you try an approach that's different from usual company practice and it *works*, you're probably in good shape. I've never known anybody who found a new way to increase company profits and succeeded in implementing his idea and as a consequence got into trouble.

But if you *fail*, at the least you won't have achieved a "plus" for your career. So you can see, there is usually some element of risk. Still, if you want to make it to the upper levels, you have to demonstrate an ability to be creative when the right opportunity presents itself.

As an illustration of this kind of corporate risk-taking, let me share an experience I had when I was the district manager for a group of Penney stores a number of years ago. One of our senior officers sent me out to one of the larger stores in the Midwest to check on a manager who had been reported to be rather "confused" because he was buying a lot of merchandise outside the normal company purchasing outlets.

My instructions were, in effect, "Seibert, you go out there and straighten this out!"

At this particular point, Penney didn't have many large stores, and some of our practices and procedures for operating urban stores were in a formative stage. This manager was operating a store in a large downtown area where he had to compete with large, well-established stores that had more experience in this type of market at the time than Penney did.

This assignment wasn't exactly ideal for me, because the store manager was many years my senior and was very likely a much better merchant than I was at that stage. But I traveled out to his store and was fully prepared to do what I had to do to solve the problem. As it turned out, the situation was somewhat different from what I had been led to expect.

My investigation revealed that the store manager was, indeed, buying some women's accessories that had not been offered or recommended by Penney. But this wasn't the result of any "confusion" on his part. When I examined the competition he was facing, I came to the same conclusion that he had: He needed more items than the company offered for that situation. Someone in the company simply didn't understand the nature of the challenge he was facing.

For instance, another large downtown department store had a women's accessories line which offered customers a much larger assortment than was then available through our company price list. If our manager had gone along with the usual company practice here, without raising any questions at all, he would not have served his customers *or* the company well.

So this Midwest store manager convinced me that he was right, and now the ball was in my court. Although it wasn't quite what my bosses were expecting, I wrote a report strongly supporting the unusual actions the store manager had taken—and stating explicitly that he was right and the existing company assortment available for a store like that one was wrong. The final result was that those in upper management bought my arguments and began to reevaluate some company assortment practices.

Now, it may seem as though this was a simple, easy problem to deal with, but it wasn't. It took courage and initiative for that store manager to allow his own creativity and the exigencies of his marketing situation to take precedence over prevalent company practice.

My own role in this situation was relatively minor and certainly didn't involve putting my whole career on the line in my decision to support a seemingly unorthodox approach to merchandising. But there was some element of risk in that I might have overlooked something in my analysis of the store manager's sales situation.

The completely safe thing to have done might have been just to side with past company practice or perhaps to give a lukewarm assessment of this man's initiative. There's always a temptation to avoid putting yourself completely on the line in support of a new idea or project. It's much easier and often seems to be safer to over-qualify your endorsement in an effort to protect your own position—just in case higher management reaches a negative conclusion about the issue.

In this illustration, the riskier thing was to give him my full support. If it had happened that for some reason I was wrong in my enthusiastic evaluation of that store, both the store manager and I might well have been in hot water. But endorsing his "maverick" decisions was the only honest and fair thing I could do—and it also turned out to be the best thing for the company.

Happily, in today's business environment, as we

think more in terms of participative or "team" management, there are better ways to express your entrepreneurial drives than taking action outside usual company programs. For example, in the above illustration, this store manager's first move might have been to notify or challenge the buyer or corporate team responsible for developing the assortment of goods that he felt he needed. This action would probably have been sufficient.

You have to take some risks and put your judgment on the line in decision-making if you expect to move up toward the top of your company. You can play it safe only up to a certain point, and then excessive timidity may begin to work against you. Those who have reached the upper plateaus of senior management have usually learned to strike a good balance between following traditional implementation of corporate programs and proposing new directions. It's a matter of developing good judgment about when a new approach is in order and then moving aggressively to convince others you're right.

But let me offer a word of caution here about the futility of innovation for its own sake: There are many ways of doing the same job, and there's no point in doing something a different way if your method isn't going to save time or money or have some other special benefit.

As one wag has said, "It doesn't make sense to invent the wheel all over again." In other words, the work on some things is already being done adequately, so don't waste your time or your company's by focusing on new approaches if existing methods are just as good.

Instead, turn your energies to other ideas or projects that will *advance* the quality of life or the size of profits. Helping your company by being exceptionally creative on the job will *always* work to your advantage in terms of enhancing your reputation and perhaps paving the way to a higher position. And sometimes outstanding creativity can have a special kind of happy surprise ending for the employee.

One good example of a "happy surprise ending" for creativity on the job involved Robert L. May, an advertising copywriter for Montgomery Ward. You've probably never heard of May, but I know you've heard of his most famous creative production—the song "Rudolph the Red-Nosed Reindeer."

May conceived of Rudolph as a promotion device for Christmas shoppers at Montgomery Ward back in 1939. Over a period of about eight years, customers were handed a booklet with a poem describing the feats of the red-nosed reindeer. Then, in recognition of May's creative achievement, the department store transferred copyright in the story to him in 1947, and the rest is history.

May first got the poem published as a book, which sold about 100,000 copies in the first year. Then May's brother-in-law, the songwriter Johnny Marks, turned the story into a song, which became a hit sung by cowboy star Gene Autry in 1949. At this writing, more than 90 million copies of about three hundred different recordings of the song have been sold.

But the important thing to remember about "Rudolph the Red-Nosed Reindeer" is that it was conceived and produced on company time by a highly creative employee of one of the nation's largest corporations. And most important of all, Robert May was a *loyal* and *honest* employee who was eager to share his idea with the company and with his fellow workers.

As far as I know, May didn't take any unusual risks in

exercising his creativity. In fact, more than most business employees, he was being *paid* to be artistically creative, so a certain level of literary achievement was expected of him.

But with an employee whose values were different from May's, the scenario in this story might have been quite different. The person could have decided, "This Rudolph concept is a great idea, but I'm not about to let anybody else get a piece of this. This is going to be mine, and mine alone." A less-than-honest person, in other words, might have taken the concept, which had been developed on company time, and tried to peddle it by himself in the public marketplace.

It's possible that another copywriter with this song in mind might have fooled his company into believing he hadn't actually developed the concept on company time. But the chances would have been astronomical against his ever achieving the kind of success that May finally did with the song.

The popularity of the booklet at Montgomery Ward gave May the kind of platform he needed to negotiate effectively with book and song publishers. Without his company behind him, he might have been just another talented songwriter trying to get a music publisher to give him a hearing. But his loyalty to his company, his willingness to work hard on the job, and the free way that he shared his creativity obviously influenced Montgomery Ward to reward him with that surprise bonus—the copyright that led to his fame and fortune.

As you consider being creative and engaging in "creative risk-taking" in your own work, it's important to understand that it's not necessary for you to be the *only* one or even the *main* one involved in the shaping of an ingenious concept or project. Robert May might have been the only one involved in creating "Rudolph the Red-Nosed Reindeer." Similarly, the store manager I was assigned to report on may have been the only one involved in the decision to order merchandise different from the usual Penney line.

But it's not always like that. In fact, when you're dealing with creativity in a majority of corporations, it's *rarely* like that. In most cases, one person may have come up with a certain idea, but then many other experts get into the act before the final product hits the stores or before the new operating procedure or policy becomes established company practice.

If it's important for you to be the only one involved in an idea, from initial conception to final implementation, then you probably don't belong in a corporation at all. But you may well find that if you try to do everything yourself, you'll fall short of what you might have accomplished if you had joined a team effort.

My own father is a good illustration of what can happen to the person who attempts to orchestrate an entire complex business project alone. He had a very original mind and was always coming up with inventions of one type or another. In fact, by the time he died, he had hundreds of patents in his name—but many of them belonged to the companies he had worked for over the years.

During the Depression, he found himself out of work, and so he decided that he would try on his own to produce and market the new ideas that came to him. Through the manufacture and sales of some of his inventions, he did manage to get the family through the Depression with enough food and clothing. But he didn't have the business skills to turn any of his ideas into big sellers.

For example, one of the best things he produced was a hard wax for automobiles. I can remember watching him work in his laboratory at home, with rows of test tubes containing alcohol, glycerine, acids, and every other substance that might cause car wax to deteriorate. He finally came up with a product that was impervious to almost everything and would last for a year or two before you had to go back for another application.

He also developed a complex machine to apply this wax, a tool about eight to ten inches long attached to a rubber-inflated device. You could apply the wax with this thing and then buff it immediately afterward. He was far ahead of his time with this invention, because all the waxes in those days were so soft they wouldn't survive a heavy rain. Also, most of the car paints were so fragile they would begin to fade soon after you bought the car. But with my dad's wax, a driver could preserve his car's paint for years.

The problem was that he didn't have any way to market this product. So he was able to sell it only in the rather limited area of Ohio near where we lived. During this entrepreneurial phase of his life, he was determined to protect all his inventions. He wanted to retain 100 percent of the rights and complete control over production and marketing. The result was that he ended up with 100 percent of a business that had relatively little value. But in retrospect, if he had been willing to share his ideas with a large company and to take even a small percentage, the results could have been much better for him.

In my father's case, the creativity in terms of the design and the engineering was there. But the marketing creativity wasn't. The beauty of exercising creativity in a corporate setting is that the skills and talents you lack may be available from others in the organization. So, many of the ideas which you can come up with on your own—but which may fall by the wayside because of certain limitations in your expertise—might well come to fruition in the context of a large company.

The old adage that two heads are better than one usually becomes a byword in a successful company, primarily because of this basic truth that creativity in business is, more often than not, a group rather than an individual phenomenon. So I would advise you to get accustomed right now, if you haven't already, to the notion of releasing your ideas to the scrutiny of your boss and your peers.

As a general rule, I believe that the more you share ideas with others, the more ideas you'll come up with. Ideas beget ideas. And the more you're willing to share, the more training you'll receive in watching a good idea become a *great* one in the process of brainstorming in business conferences.

Up to this point, we've discussed several types of creativity, some of which involve more risk-taking than others. But there is one kind of creative risk-taking that is especially dangerous—and may even be the first step toward the loss of your job if you're not careful. I'm referring to actions by employees that violate established company policies or firm guidelines. If you break the government's law you may well be fined or end up in jail. If you break the established "laws" in a corporation, you probably won't end up behind bars—but you'll definitely increase your chances of ending up on the street without a job.

Let me illustrate this point with an incident from my own experience—an action I took as a young assistant store manager which, as I look back on it, could only be described as a dumb move. If I had been doing only an average job in my work at the time, I could have seriously hurt my position in the Penney Company.

A directive had come down while I was working in this store that everybody in the store except the manager had to record his hours on a time clock. I was working long hours at the time—about seventy-five hours a week—and I had a large staff under me. Somehow, it just didn't seem right for the company to require me to be treated like more junior employees who worked by the hour. I had worked long and hard to get to my present position, and I considered myself to be part of the management team. As a matter of fact, if I hadn't been on the management team, no one else would have been either, except perhaps for the store manager himself.

Other people in my position might not have minded this requirement, but for me it was a matter of personal dignity and integrity. I decided that if this company had promoted me to assistant store manager, I was going to act like a manager. So I refused to punch the clock.

The manager was rather amused at first by the issue I had raised. But he said, "Look, this is company policy. We have to do it. Auditors will be coming in, looking at who's working and what their hours were, and you'll get in trouble if you don't do it."

But still, I refused. I had decided to take my stand on this point—no matter how trivial the issue might seem to anybody else. Eventually, the store manager just threw up his hands and dropped the whole thing—and I never punched a time clock from then on. As I look back on it, I realize I could have lost my job over this incident, but I was lucky.

So there are dangers in this sort of decision. If you choose to defy a company policy that relates only to your own dignity and has nothing to do with helping the company improve its profits, you're definitely skating on thin ice. Even if you manage to keep your job, you may find yourself getting a poor recommendation from your current employers when you are looking for another job later on.

I'm reminded of an incident involving a reporter on a large urban newspaper. In this case, the reporter had fallen into the habit of openly criticizing his editors and other top managers. Finally, the fellow quit, and on his last day of work, he stood at the back of the city room, shouted obscenities about the paper at the top of his lungs, and then stalked out.

This erratic outburst may have made him feel good temporarily. But if I had been his boss, I couldn't have imagined giving him any sort of decent recommendation to prospective employers. I would have felt a responsibility not to inflict him, with his distasteful behavior, on any other company.

So you have to know where to draw the line between what is acceptable nonconformity that establishes your own dignity, integrity, and creativity, and what is silly or unprofessional behavior. In retrospect, for instance, I know I didn't do the right thing in that time-clock incident. At the time, it seemed very important to me to take the risk in order to make my point. In reality, however, the point I was making centered more on satisfying my own ego than on doing something creative to help the company.

But even though I obviously took more of a risk than was warranted in my effort to assert what I perceived as my rights, the line between creativity and conformity in business is not always so clear. In this chapter, we've examined a number of cases where risk-taking to one degree or another is quite appropriate in expressing your ideas and putting your special stamp on company practices and operations. But now, let's focus on the other side of the coin—the myths and realities of corporate conformity.

CHAPTER 7
A VOTE *for* CORPORATE CONFORMITY

When I was on a business trip overseas a number of years ago, I had the opportunity to visit the offices of a corporation in Madrid. The Madrid business community tends to be rather formal, so I was quite surprised to see that none of the men in the office wore a necktie. Even the top executive, who had asked me out to lunch to cap our business discussions, though he was very neatly and stylishly dressed, wasn't wearing a tie.

Curious at the breach of normal business custom, I asked this officer, "Did I happen to arrive here on some sort of company holiday? I've noticed nobody in your office is wearing a tie."

"No, it's not a holiday," he replied. "I don't permit neckties in our offices."

"What do you mean?"

"Just what I said. I believe that a tie is an inhibiting influence on a person's ability to think and produce. It's a barrier to productive management. It's like putting a collar on an animal."

Somewhat disconcerted, I asked, "Has this ever created any kind of a problem for you?"

"Only one that I can think of," he said. "A few years ago, I hired a man from one of the local banks who was in his forties and had been wearing a tie to work for more than twenty years. When I told him he wouldn't be allowed to wear a tie anymore, he had some trouble adjusting. In fact, he was quite disturbed and had to start going for psychiatric treatments to regain his ability to function. Somehow, he didn't feel he looked like an executive without his tie. But the psychiatrist got him straightened out, and he's doing fine now. Of course, he comes to work with an open-neck shirt like everyone else."

I was still mulling over this novel approach to corporate attire when we arrived at the country club where this executive had planned for us to eat. It suddenly dawned on me, as we walked toward the dining room, that this place required a coat *and* tie, and I started to point out this difficulty to my host.

But before I could get a word out, his hand was in his coat pocket and he had produced a rumpled necktie, already knotted, and slipped it over his head. The tie was arranged so that the thin part hung well below the wide part, and the knot dangled in a loose arc below the man's unbuttoned shirt.

Altogether, the total image was ludicrous. But he had satisfied the requirement that members and their guests wear a tie—and at the same time, he was making a statement that he felt their rule was silly.

I've turned this experience over in my mind many times, because, even though it's a true story, it also serves as something of a parable about conformity in the business world. For this Spanish executive, the normal requirements of corporate dress had so deeply offended him that he had made a major issue out of a relatively unimportant set of business customs. In effect, he had gone full circle and ended up falling into the very trap he so deplored. He had set his own standard of dress and forced his employees to conform to his special brand of nonconformity.

Conformity and nonconformity are relative concepts, and usually, in my opinion, it's not worth making an issue out of common customs in dress or behavior that have grown up over the years in any given company. If corporate conformity becomes so oppressive that it threatens to stifle your creativity, then that's unacceptable. But in most cases, doing the customary thing just helps you do a better job and results in one fewer obstacle to get in the way of your relationships with your peers and supervisors.

This whole question of corporate conformity is especially important because it's intimately tied up with the concept of leadership in business. If you're going to succeed, you have to be a leader, and that means you have to stay out in front of your peers—but not too far out front! If you're operating in a completely different dimension, as the ultimate maverick, it won't make any difference how talented or creative you are, because when you glance back over your shoulder, you'll find nobody is following you.

A successful businessperson knows how to conform to company customs—including dress and behavior—so that other workers feel comfortable identifying with him. But at the same time, he knows when and how to step ahead of the pack and draw them along with him.

This is another way of saying that you should strive to become a special kind of model for others—the best representative of the entire group, on the cutting edge of beneficial change but not so unorthodox in your appearance or habits that you project a bizarre rather than businesslike image.

Many people demonstrate leadership qualities at a very young age, but frequently they are flashes in the pan. They may become the captains of athletic teams or presidents of school organizations. But they don't follow up and build on their early successes. To reach the upper levels in business, it's not essential that you show a pattern of *super* leadership at some point in life—just that you've had experience in guiding others and that you have the patience and persistence to build on it.

Think back on your own experiences in the past in different organizations. For example, when you were in high school or college, there was undoubtedly at least one organization in which you were an officer or took some leadership role. Perhaps you have also served as the head of some church or synagogue committee, or a community group or social organization. Whatever your background in taking charge of others, you can develop those latent leadership skills into a potent force if you just set your mind to it.

In some respects, the best leader is the best conformist. But "conformity," as I'm using the term, refers more to the way a person acts or looks than to the way he thinks. Nothing I'm saying here should be taken to mean that the individual should try to restrict his inner creative impulses and thought patterns. On the contrary, the most effective leadership abilities can often be traced back to a faculty for looking at problems and situations a little differently than everybody else does—and then convincing others that they should follow your approach.

Here are a few ways I've discovered to conform to company custom—and yet use that conformity as a springboard for effective leadership in developing new, creative business methods and corporate policies:

—You have to understand your business thoroughly. If you develop superior knowledge of every aspect of the tasks assigned to you, you'll find people coming to you, asking for advice. Also, people will begin to want to work for you because they'll know you're acquiring a good reputation in the company as a highly productive employee.

—You have to make yourself available to others and be willing to teach them and assist them as they develop their skills. If you become stingy with your knowledge, perhaps because of a fear that somebody else may get to be as good as you are, you'll never become a real leader. Instead, you may develop the reputation of being a person who is paranoid, egocentric, and in the last analysis downright unfriendly!

—It's wise to follow most reasonable company traditions involving such things as dress and general behavior—even if at first they seem rather superficial and unimportant to you. One reason for this approach is that certain things about your job may be worth fighting for or against, but certain other things are definitely not. If you accept a job with a particular company which stresses certain customs, then you should be ready to conform to those customs—or find another job!

For example, IBM used to have a custom that its employees would wear suits and *white* shirts—no pastels or colors. If you want to work in a specific company and a certain dress code like this is a prerequisite for being fully accepted by management, then you'd better be willing to conform, or find a job more in line with your personal tastes.

Of course, there are people who feel they have to make a big issue out of company traditions like this. I know of one very talented manager who decided to stick it out and buck tradition in a company which also had a rather strict dress code. This man had a heavy beard and a penchant for casual western clothes. But unfortunately, his superiors weren't too sympathetic to the personal appearance he had chosen.

At first, in the early stages of his movement upward in the company, he was regarded merely as a lovable eccentric. Everybody kidded him and even enjoyed having him around. But when his expertise helped him move up to the middle management levels, he began to become a source of embarrassment. In fact, some of his superiors became reluctant to invite him to meetings with executives from other companies, because they felt the image he projected did his company more harm than good.

So here you have a man whose outstanding skills enabled him to move up to a responsible position in his corporation, but whose nonconformity placed a definite ceiling on his ability to keep moving toward the top. A couple of senior executives finally took him aside to explain how his mode of dress was hurting him, but he became offended and refused to listen to them. In other words, his need to be different in some way ran so deep that he was willing to sacrifice his career in order to maintain his differences.

Now, I couldn't begin to sort through the various psychological motives and personal values that would prompt a man like that to make the choices he did. In my opinion, he picked a minor, unimportant issue on which to take his stand. I would personally have preferred to put my western clothes in the closet and start wearing pinstripe suits if such conformity of dress would open some doors for me on the way to the upper levels of the company. If I am going to take a firm stand on anything,

I'd rather do it on a matter of creativity or personal integrity. But that becomes a matter of individual choice about what's true and important in life and what's not.

The same kinds of considerations apply with many other types of business customs and traditions. And in these other situations, as with questions of proper clothing, it's also important to know where to draw the line between those practices you should follow and those you can safely disregard. The line is different in every company, so in the final analysis it's up to you to size up your own position and make your personal decisions accordingly.

For example, you'll probably find that when management people start talking among themselves, there will be advice tossed about concerning such things as the best clubs to belong to or the preferred sections of town to look for a home. Sometimes, this "management scuttlebutt" may provide some valid guidance for you. Thus, if in your job you're expected to entertain clients regularly in your home, it wouldn't make much sense to select a place far out of town with a tiny dining room that was inconvenient for guests.

On the other hand, if you buy an extremely expensive home on a relatively modest middle management salary primarily so that you can "be with the right class of people"—and perhaps give your bosses the impression that you're top-management material because you *live* like a top manager—you're probably wasting your time and your money. Also, if you begin to run into financial problems because you've spent too much money trying to emulate a supposed "executive life-style," it's likely that your superiors will begin to question your judgment.

If you run down most "requirements" or "customs"

related to housing or club memberships for junior executives, you'll probably find they aren't requirements or customs at all. More often than not, they're figments in the imagination of other middle managers.

In the final analysis, it's essential to maintain an ongoing evaluation of what your ultimate priorities are in life and business. Where should you compromise and conform, and where should you dare to be different?

As your personal value system matures over the years, you'll find yourself shrugging at many corporate practices, like dress customs, and you'll wonder how you could ever have considered bucking the trend on such trivial matters.

With the development of this maturity, you'll probably conform in most ways, because there are usually good reasons why those customs or practices have developed. Also, it's often not worth putting yourself on the line and playing the maverick on minor issues that won't advance you in the company. As a result, the majority of your fellow workers and your superiors will come to recognize you as a "company man" or a "company woman"—in the best sense of those terms.

Then, with this reputation solidly undergirding you, you'll be poised to step away from the pack and to exercise your creative drive in a way that will establish you as a true leader among those who are most loyal to the company. The specific ways in which you can begin to make yourself stand out from your peers—and also establish yourself as a high achiever and leader in the eyes of your boss—are the next topic we want to explore.

CHAPTER 8

The HIGH-ACHIEVER IMAGE

The junior executive burst through the door of her boss's office five minutes late, with papers practically falling out of her briefcase and the collar of her coat jacket turned under the wrong way. She piled part of her materials down on the edge of his desk, dropped down in a chair in front of him, and started rattling off her report in such a breathless, disorganized way that he had to stop her frequently to find out exactly what she was talking about.

When their session was finally completed and they were both on their way to the elevators, the supervisor tried to set her at ease with some casual conversation: "Did you notice that editorial on inflation in the *Wall Street Journal* today?"

But she hadn't noticed because she hadn't even bought a newspaper that morning.

This young woman—a real person who actually did have this encounter with a supervisor—violated almost every principle associated with what might be called the "high-achiever image." In some ways, this image or personality, which every successful executive must possess to one degree or another, is related to our discussion of corporate conformity in the preceding chapter—but there's one crucial difference.

Some degree of conformity to general company policy and practice is necessary if you hope to be accepted as "one of the guys," or a member in good standing of the corporate family you've chosen. But your image can't be restricted to the lowest common denominator that identifies your fellow employees. In some way, you have to stand out. You have to develop an image that will make your supervisors see you as more efficient and more competent than the average worker.

In some respects, I know that by opening this subject to discussion I could be misunderstood to be emphasizing mere appearance rather than solid substance. And I'll readily concede that I'm going to concentrate on outward impressions and image right now. But I don't in any way believe that cultivating an effective, successful image is inconsistent with being a highly effective worker. Far from it! As a matter of fact, developing an impressive high-achiever image can make you a much stronger manager.

As I said, the junior executive pictured at the beginning of this chapter projects the antithesis of the image of the high achiever who shows great promise for future success. But what exactly was she doing wrong? Some of her mistakes are obvious, but others may not be so apparent. So I'd like to spend some time analyzing exactly what she did incorrectly and how you can learn from her mistakes.

Generally speaking, there are at least four keys that will get you into the company of the "comers" in your corporation. Your ability to perform is always the main factor that will help move you into the elite group of upwardly mobile managers. But you also have to communicate to your bosses the message "I'm executive material," and that means understanding and using these four basic keys:

1. Broad general reading habits.

You'll recall that while the junior executive and her boss were moving toward the elevator, the boss tried to start a conversation about a newspaper item. But the young woman hadn't read the paper that day. This interchange points up a basic characteristic in the corporate high achiever—being well-read on a variety of current subjects.

I can't give you any absolute rules about what you should read to succeed in business. But let me suggest a few guidelines that may be helpful in enhancing your successful image. First of all, let's consider how much time you should spend in reading peripheral matters each day—i.e., *not* business correspondence or other required on-the-job reading, but such things as newspapers, magazines, and books.

For example, I spend a couple of hours every day on this "outside" reading. If I'm traveling by train or airplane, I often read and scan this sort of material from departure to arrival. When I'm on vacation, I devote two to three hours each day to general reading.

Obviously, my personal habits won't be applicable to many other people, because each of us has a different schedule and a different set of outside commitments. But the main point here is that it's important to do some significant amount of outside reading: Don't skimp on it!

What exactly should you read?

I recommend three newspapers—the *Wall Street Journal*, a general national newspaper like the *New York Times* or the *Washington Post*, and a local newspaper. If you're pressed for time, you might concentrate on the front page, editorial page, and financial section of these papers, because those are the parts that are most likely to be useful in a business discussion. In many business lunches or other meetings, you're at a disadvantage if you can't respond to comments or questions your colleagues or superiors may have about current news items. Also, if you display ignorance on small topics such as news items that are relevant to your business, it may suggest a general lack of preparation on your part.

As for magazines, I would pick one of the three major weekly newsmagazines to read each week—*Time*, *Newsweek*, or *U.S. News & World Report*. Also, you should probably read at least one, and preferably more, of the general-interest business publications, such as *Fortune*, *Business Week*, and *Forbes*.

These business magazines keep you abreast of trends and also personalities in different fields. So if you're reading them regularly, you'll be more likely to know something about a wide variety of topics when they come up in conversation.

Let me offer one word of advice, though: You should read *all* these publications with a critical eye. Some magazines or writers will in effect do an overly positive public-relations job for certain executives or industries. Other publications will go to the other extreme, with an unbalanced hatchet job on some individual or company.

If you cite facts or opinions that you've gleaned from a journalistic source, be sure you attribute it to that source, and don't immediately accept it as gospel. Otherwise, you may end up with the proverbial egg on your face during a conversation with someone who has more inside information than your journalistic authority.

After you've read most publications over a period of months and years, you'll also find you can begin to identify latent biases and superficial reporting. As a result, you'll have a much more accurate and balanced foundation of information on which to base many of your business discussions and decisions.

I know, by the way, that the outside reading I'm suggesting you do may seem overwhelming at first. But there are some very helpful techniques that can help you to consume more information in a shorter period of time. If you're particularly ambitious, you might take one of the established speed-reading courses. I know a number of executives who have benefited dramatically from this sort of instruction.

If you don't have the time or inclination to take a formal course, you should at least practice techniques of scanning—something I've found to be especially helpful in my own reading. In a newspaper, for example, you might read the first three or four paragraphs of news stories you're interested in, and then glance over the first sentence of each remaining paragraph and also the other highlights that catch your eye.

This approach works quite well with news stories—or those which report breaking, daily events—because this type of writing is written with the most important information in the first couple of paragraphs. The next most important items come in the following few paragraphs, and so on down to the least important material at the end of the story. Newspaper writers are instructed to write their stories this way, in order of declining importance of subject matter, so that their editors can lop off some of the less important paragraphs at the end if they run out of space during printing.

Unlike news stories, feature articles and editorials are often researched and written well in advance of the date of publication. They usually have a clear-cut introduction, body, and conclusion, and, as a result, you should read the last couple of paragraphs as closely as the first to pick up any concluding points that the writer may have had in mind.

Using a proper scanning technique, you'll probably find you can go through the highlights of the *Wall Street Journal* in about ten minutes—certainly a manageable task for anyone before work each morning. If the junior executive at the first of this chapter had taken a few minutes for this discipline, she would have had plenty to talk about with her boss as they walked to the elevators, and she would definitely have made a better impression on him.

Up to this point, I haven't mentioned much at all about books, but that's not because I don't consider them important. As a matter of fact, it's not at all uncommon for a business executive to mention a best-seller or popular business volume he's reading. If you know something about the topic too, you'll be able to establish yourself as a well-read person who can bring a broad base of knowledge to a job.

Of course, none of this reading of newspapers, magazines, or books should be pursued merely to make yourself look good to your superiors. There are much more substantive considerations involved than that. In the first place, the more you know, the better you'll be able to perform on your job and the more effective you'll become in conversations with your fellow workers.

With books, especially, you'll find the benefits center on broadening your knowledge and in sharpening all the communications skills you use on the job. In other words, it isn't a matter of turning yourself overnight into a whiz of a conversationalist. In many cases, the books you're reading won't be exactly the books your boss or colleagues are into at that particular moment. But the more books you get under your belt, the more powerful your conversational ability will become, until after several months or years of following active reading habits, you'll find you have something significant to say about almost every topic that comes up in ordinary conversation.

I've been asked what I consider to be the most significant books I've read. That's a hard question to answer, because different books have been very important to me at different points in my life. But I have developed a kind of overall reading plan which you might find helpful. Here are the most important books or categories of books and a few comments about how they have been particularly significant in my own business experience.

• **The dictionary.** Many people I know give lip service to the importance of having a dictionary at hand when they come across an unfamiliar word. But as a practical matter, they never refer to it.

There are so many words in the English language and so many nuances of meaning that you're sure to misuse words unless you constantly check their precise definitions in a dictionary. And if you do make a mistake, either in a written report or letter or in an oral exchange, you're going to place yourself at a disadvantage.

One of the best ways to put the brakes on your upward mobility in a company is to get the reputation of being a Mrs. (or Mr.) Malaprop—one who regularly misuses words, as did the comic female character in Sheridan's play *The Rivals*.

The problem here is not only that you may appear to be ignorant or lacking in education. Another, and perhaps more serious, objection to misusing words is that this flaw gets in the way of effective communication. Those who hear you make a grammatical error or use the wrong word will tend to focus briefly on the mistake and not on the subsequent things you have to say. But the slight gap in their attentiveness may well prevent them from picking up some very important points you're making.

I myself have had to pull people aside after they've made a presentation and ask them to repeat something—simply because they made some disconcerting error, like putting a sentence together awkwardly, which I then started thinking about instead of their talk. So it's extremely important to make regular use of a dictionary and perhaps even tools like grammar books, because no matter how good your ideas may be, they will never get off the ground unless you can get them across in accurate, compelling language.

• **A thesaurus.** This reference book can inject some variety into your vocabulary by helping you find a word quickly when you're stumped because the word you want has temporarily escaped you. A thesaurus, which contains both synonyms and antonyms for thousands of words, can help you break literary logjams when you're working on a speech or doing any other form of writing.

• **Practical management books.** A wide variety of books in this genre are constantly being published, and I would strongly recommend that you browse periodically through your local bookstore and pick up any that can fill in some of the cracks in your knowledge. Peter Drucker's *Management: Tasks, Practices, Responsibilites* is one of the classics and should be on your reading list if you haven't already gone through it. As you move through Drucker's volume or some other text that happens to catch your eye, you'll find you occasionally come across concepts and advice that you already know. The knowledge that you already possess some of the information that an expert is presenting should give you some confidence about your progress. But you'll also probably find there's a great deal you don't know, and so you'll soon realize the time you're spending on a book like *Management* is definitely worthwhile.

• **Histories of corporations or businesses.** When you're in the lower or middle levels of a particular company, sometimes it's hard to see the forest for the trees. You may know your specific job quite well, but you may also have a sense you don't have a grasp of the "big picture." For example, perhaps you really can't understand how a certain staff job complements a particular sales position. Reading a book like Alfred Sloan's *My Years with General Motors* can give you a broad view of many aspects of a large company. And even if the corporation you're reading about isn't your own, you'll develop some reference points to develop a better understanding of your own job.

• **Biographies.** I find almost any well-researched biography on a famous person to be instructive in my own personal development. For example, it's always helpful to study the strengths and weaknesses of a monumental figure like General Douglas MacArthur, as depicted in a book like *American Caesar: Douglas MacArthur 1880-1964*, by William Manchester. But even though biographies may help the reader profit by the mistakes and learn from the accomplishments of others, this type of book does have some clear shortcomings. There are biases built into any book, and biographies are no exception. It's very hard to get into somebody else's head successfully and really understand what caused the person to do certain things. So my advice would be this: Read *many* biographies, and compare them with one another—and with real life. Then you'll have a broader, more accurate picture of what any given author is trying to say about a particular public figure, and you'll be in a better position to choose those lessons to learn and features to emulate.

• **Historical fiction.** This is a very personal preference of mine, but I do feel there is a great deal to be learned from well-researched novels that deal with major historical figures and events. After I read Herman Wouk's books on World War II, *Winds of War* and *War and Remembrance*, I felt I had a much deeper understanding of the interaction between personality development and major historical events—an understanding that a strictly factual account couldn't give me. In a distinctive way available through no other artistic or journalistic medium, many good novels can broaden your perspective of what's going on at other levels of society and other parts of the country and the world. But let me add one final note about fiction: There's nothing wrong with the upwardly mobile person who occasionally reads purely for recreation! In fact, there's a lot that's *right* about it, because sitting down with a light detective story or western can be tremendously relaxing and refreshing. Of course, there's always the chance that you'll find something in one of Louis L'Amour's gunfighters or Eric Ambler's spies that you can use as an illustration in a speech or other presentation. But the utilitarian value may be peripheral; the important thing is to come away from a good read in a more positive, alert frame of mind.

• **The Bible.** I try to read some passages from the Bible every day, primarily because it's the key source of spiritual authority in my life. As a businessman, I've been particularly impressed with the relevance to my work experience of two books of the Bible, Proverbs and the Gospel of Matthew. Proverbs is replete with references to the proper approach to business transactions, such as "A wicked man earns deceptive wages, but one who sows righteousness gets a sure reward" (11:18, RSV). And Jesus' teachings and parables in Matthew have enough practical wisdom in them to provide a blueprint for almost an entire working experience (e.g., Matthew 5-7; 21:28-41; 25:14-30).

As I've said, this reading plan is a very personal thing which has worked for me for a number of years now, and I'm well aware that some of the specifics may not be appropriate for others. But I do feel strongly that it's necessary for you to begin *some sort* of outside reading program so that you understand your job against a broader context. Also, the more you read, the better prepared you'll be to participate intelligently when your discussions at work drift away from the particular tasks at hand.

With just a minimal amount of time set aside for newspapers each day, you'll most likely never get caught in the awkward position of that junior executive who was at a loss for words when her boss tried to strike up a casual conversation about current events.

2. Advance preparation.

Now let's take a look at another aspect of the encounter of our junior executive with her boss. When she entered his office, she obviously looked as though she had been working hard on her assignment, with all those papers falling out of her briefcase. And after the supervisor took the lead and helped her organize her presentation on the spot, it became evident that she had indeed done a great deal of advance preparation.

The problem, though, was that she failed to pay attention to preparing the *image* she wanted to convey to him. As a result, she gave the impression of being completely disorganized—and in fact, she *was* disorganized, even though in one sense she was also well prepared.

I've found over the years that it's absolutely essential to set a deadline well in advance of a formal presentation or a discussion with your boss so that you'll have a "buffer" of time in which to collect your thoughts and put the final polish on your personal appearance and the organization of your presentation. Or to say it another way, you should avoid continuing your research and report-drafting right up to the final minute before you have to make a presentation.

For most people it's essential to set aside at least a few minutes, and sometimes half an hour or more, depending on the complexity of your report, to allow time to become calm and to focus on the key points you want to make. Then, when you walk into the conference room or office where you're scheduled to convey your information, you'll be able to start right off with your most important points, rather than waste time on irrelevant or peripheral material. If your boss has to organize your presentation for you on the spot, you'll fail to capitalize fully on an opportunity to put your best foot forward.

Also, it's helpful to use the buffer time you've set aside to go to the restroom and check your physical appearance. Is your hair combed, your lipstick on straight, your tie neat? If you look windblown or harried when you walk through your supervisors's door, you may distract his attention from the message you're trying to get across.

Another important facet of advance preparation is *punctuality*. If you're expected to be at a meeting at 10:00 a.m., you should be there by that time, not five or ten minutes later. In fact, it's a good idea to get to the appointed place a few minutes early so that you're ready and waiting when your boss enters the room.

I've been guilty of violating this principle myself on occasion, but I think there's rarely any excuse for it. When you're five minutes late, you've in effect stolen that five minutes from the other person, and his time is at least as valuable to him as yours is to you. And if it's your boss's time you're stealing—as was the case in the example we're using—his time is definitely more important in terms of hard dollars and cents because he's getting paid at a higher rate. In any case, if your supervisor becomes annoyed with you, that's a poor way to start any meeting.

Proper advance preparation also involves *anticipation*. At some point during your preliminary work, you need to step back for a moment and ask yourself, "Have I covered everything? What questions are likely to be raised by my presentation?"

You can give the appearance of having done a rather superficial job unless you've jotted down possible objections or questions about your work and then come up with some reasonable, well-documented responses. This anticipation technique can be quite helpful in developing your management skills.

Of course, you can never anticipate *every* question you may be asked, but good preparation will help you even with those queries that you may not have been expecting. I've known a number of highly intelligent, conscientious young executives who have been caught flat-footed by an unusual point in a discussion but who were still able to come out of the meeting looking good—both because of their generally sound preparation and also because of their intellectual honesty.

They didn't try to bluff their way through an answer and pretend they knew more than they did. Instead, they might respond, "Frankly, I haven't thought through this issue completely yet, but here's a reaction off the top of my head. . . ." Having laid the groundwork for an impromptu, shoot-from-the-hip response, they were somewhat protected if their answer happened to be wrong or inadequate. But they also put themselves in a position to shine even more brightly if they hit upon just the right thought.

This principle of preparing for encounters and questions with your bosses will continue to apply no matter how high you go in your company. You might think that as chief executive officer, I don't have to worry about such things as answering to people and being prepared for questions that may be put to me in business meetings. But actually, I have at least as much pressure to get ready for certain meetings and challenges as I ever have had—especially when the annual shareholders' meeting rolls around.

I spend days reading relevant materials and studying hundreds of potential questions before the sessions with the stockholders. Typically, I'm asked only fifteen or twenty questions at those meetings, and most of those may have nothing to do with the specific questions I've studied. But even though 99 percent of the things I've pored over won't come up in the meeting, I know my preparation gives me a better information base for my other work in the months ahead.

For example, there is the news conference following the shareholders' meetings, where some of the material I've prepared *may* become an issue. There will also be meetings with securities analysts and interviews with media representatives.

3. Persuasive written and oral style.

In meetings I've had with business-school representatives, I've been asked, "How can we improve our curriculum?" My response is fairly consistent: I always tell them that the biggest deficiency I see in many graduates is that they lack the ability to write and also to express themselves orally.

If you can't communicate your ideas, it doesn't make much difference how good those ideas are. So one of the main things you should concentrate on as you make your way up the ladder is your skill in getting your thoughts across clearly on paper and in conversations.

As far as your writing ability is concerned, I'm not going to spend much time talking about how to write a coherent sentence or a good business report. There are plenty of complete books on that subject, and I'll leave it to you to do some independent study in this area if you feel you need improvement. (Frankly, I don't know anyone who can't use some improvement in his writing skills!) One particularly helpful short book on how to write clearly is *The Elements of Style* by William Strunk, Jr., and E.B. White, and you'll find plenty of others in your library or local bookstore.

I want to spend a little more time on how to communicate orally in a business setting, because I find it's much harder to get good materials on this subject than on improving your writing. Most of the principles I'm going to discuss here apply whether you're making a report to one supervisor or to a larger group.

First of all, I always reduce every report to writing before I try to deliver it orally. The reason for this is that it's important to be able to study and evaluate exactly what it is you have to say—whether it makes sense, runs on too long, or is really persuasive. One big mistake many people make is to try to cover too much ground in too short a period of time. Once you've committed your thoughts to paper, it's much easier to get a feel for whether you've bitten off more than you can chew in the allotted time. Also, this written phase of your report doesn't have to be a tightly written composition unless you're *required* to turn in a written report. An extended outline will do just as well.

An important side benefit of putting your thoughts down on paper is that you'll be able to see more clearly whether you've completed your homework. When you go in to present some topic to your boss or a group, you should always know more about the subject than they do. Seeing what you've researched in black and white in front of you will help you determine whether or not you need to do some final work before you go in for your presentation.

When you begin to make your oral report, keep your sentences short and your vocabularly clear and simple. One of the worst things you can do is to try to impress your boss with four-syllable words. If he doesn't understand what you're saying, it's more likely he'll get annoyed rather than be impressed.

It's a good idea to go over your oral presentation several times before you actually give it. In doing this, you'll often find opportunities to improve the way the material is organized, and you'll also be more certain of conveying all the points you want to make. In addition, you may discover some weaknesses in the way you've prepared your thoughts. It's very disappointing to make an oral presentation and then later on, when you get back to your office, realize you've left something important out. And that can certainly happen if you fail to rehearse what you plan to say. Going back to our original example of the young female executive, you can infer that she got caught in this problem of inadequate rehearsals.

But there's more to be said about this rehearsal concept: Many people don't realize that even with much experience, the dynamics of a situation can influence what you say or how articulate you are. It may not be that you're nervous or intimidated, but being in a room with an audience is different from thinking in private about what you're going to say. In the first place, your concentration is different. When you're in a group, you have to read their reactions and be prepared to have them interrupt you with questions. It's easy to drift away from where you want to be.

Part of this problem of operating in front of a real group can be overcome by experience. And part of it can be overcome by a "dress rehearsal" ahead of time, in which you give the presentation out loud in front of a colleague—or perhaps even your spouse. If you settle on this latter approach, you might ask the people who have agreed to listen to point out areas they find confusing or unclear. If your spouse or friend doesn't have time to listen to a thirty-minute presentation, you can still gain a great deal of benefit by summarizing your main points in five minutes or so and then soliciting comments and criticisms. With this sort of preparation, the final product you present to your boss should be considerably more effective.

Relying on an outsider in this way will force you to simplify and clarify even the most difficult and complex sections of your report. And I can assure you that your boss will be much happier with your presentation—especially if the materials are highly technical. Most general managers can comprehend the technical information under their supervision, but they often don't have time to keep up with all the minute details of this computer program or that direct-mail test. They usually want to understand your main points, but they don't need every little bit of trivia you've encountered in your research. So you must learn to home in on the key issues and then become expert at presenting them in a clear, hard-hitting way.

But an important qualification must be mentioned here. I'm not suggesting that you should ignore the details of your job or skim over technical matters that may be central to the production of a high-quality product. You have to be on top of the subject as much as possible when you go in for your oral report. Also—just as I do with our annual stockholders' meetings—you should be ready to answer many more questions than will ever be put to you. Otherwise, you may be embarrassed when you encounter an executive who does have more of an interest in asking technical questions.

Let me suggest one rather effective approach to giving a highly technical report to a diverse group of executives, some with technical expertise and some without. In such a situation, I would still simplify the material as much as possible for the basic oral report. But at the same time, I would bring into the room all of my technical papers, studies, and charts which relate to the report. This approach would put me in a position to support any in-depth answer I might be asked to give, and also would clearly signal that I was thoroughly prepared.

Of course, sometimes people will bring in more material than necessary, simply to impress the audience. This is a dangerous thing to do, because you may be asked a question about one of these pieces of research and you may not be familiar with it. So if you are asked about one of those volumes you've so ostentatiously brought in, you'd certainly better be able to respond with a coherent answer. Otherwise, your arming yourself with these tomes may be perceived as a mere bluff, and you could be opening yourself up to considerable embarrassment.

Before we leave this topic of how to give clear oral

presentations, there are two other important issues we should touch upon—the use of visual aids in oral reports, and the best way to handle questions and dialogue from the floor.

Many oral reports at business meetings involve the use of charts, pictures, or slides, so it's important for you to become comfortable using these devices. I tried a number of ways to employ these visual aids, and I found many of them difficult to work into my presentation until I hit upon a technique that works very well for me.

Instead of writing out a complete script and then developing slides and charts to support it, I now develop a preliminary outline first. Then I plan the visual materials before I do any more writing. Finally, when I have the finished graphs and slides I want, I sit down and write my report around those visual aids. The visual materials, rather than the words I plan to speak, thus become the focal point for my presentation, and the whole report comes across as being much clearer and better organized. This method also saves time, because you eliminate the need to rewrite the speech completely after you receive the slides.

But there are always some potential dangers that accompany slide presentations: If you're preparing a speech that includes a lot of slides, you can expect people to keep their eyes glued on the screen. I've been at talks where a slide stayed on for two minutes and people continued to stare at it, even though they had already digested it thoroughly in the first few seconds. They became almost transfixed by the screen. This problem can be compounded if the slide is complicated and requires a great deal of reading, because you can be sure if a listener is studying your slide, he's not listening to what you have to say.

So it's important to use slides carefully and avoid leaving them on any longer than necessary. The visual element in a presentation will always take precedence in people's minds over the oral. As a result, if you want people to concentrate primarily on what you're saying, it's necessary (1) to keep slides simple and easy to understand and (2) to project them on the screen only for limited periods of time.

But no matter how good your basic oral presentation, you haven't completed communicating until you have fielded questions effectively from the floor. The best kind of presentation is one which involves some sort of dialogue with your audience. The main reason for the importance of such interaction is that participation and involvement tend to raise the level of understanding and retention.

A fundamental principle in receiving questions from your audience is to establish ground rules at the beginning of the presentation. If you want your listeners to interrupt you during your talk, then tell them so right at the outset. But if you've prepared in such a way that it will be disruptive for any interruptions to come before you finish, ask them to hold their queries until you finish. Otherwise, you may find yourself being hit with a question just as you're building up to a major point, and the answer to the question, if you give it immediately, can spoil the continuity or reduce the impact of the point you're trying to make.

It takes most people a fair amount of practice before they become really adept at answering questions from the floor. But the better prepared you are for each talk and the more experience you acquire in this dialogue form of presentation, the more convinced you'll become of how useful it can be.

I should mention that sometimes you don't have any choice about when the questions will be put to you. There are at least two important situations that may confront you in this regard. First of all, when you go in for a one-on-one talk with your boss, you obviously don't have complete control over what develops, and you'll just have to "go with the flow" of the conversation. For instance, you may have a ten- or fifteen-minute presentation put together, but your boss may start getting fidgety after a couple of minutes and begin to break in with questions that concern him. As a result, the rest of your report may have to be conveyed through a quasi-dialogue. This sort of unexpected interruption may unnerve you at first, but I regard challenges like this as extremely valuable, because they give you a chance to develop your verbal skills under tough circumstances.

The second case involves a presentation before a larger group, and in that case you may be able to exercise a little more control than you can during a meeting with a single supervisor. The reason that you're more powerful in the larger-group situation—even if you're the junior person present—is that the individual who has the responsibility to take the lead in making a group presentation automatically is invested with more authority than he would otherwise command.

So if you're asked a question that you plan to cover at a later point in your report, it's entirely appropriate to indicate that fact (whereas if you were in a meeting with a single supervisor, you might come across as being a little arrogant if you told him to hold his questions until you'd finished). In a group session, for example, you might just say, "That's a good question, but if you don't mind, I'd like to answer it later in my prepared material."

4. Appropriate body language.

If you can develop good control over your bodily movements and facial expressions during personal encounters with your bosses, you'll improve your image as an up-and-coming executive. I should say at the outset of this discussion that I'm not suggesting it will be a disaster if you get a little nervous before an important meeting or encounter with a supervisor. On the contrary, I don't think twice about a young person who has damp palms when we shake hands, or who has a few beads of perspiration on the forehead, or perhaps a quavering voice. Almost everybody has been through this sort of discomfort, and there are few experienced supervisors who would write you off just because you're a little edgy or nervous.

But there are other physical mannerisms that can definitely work against you, and it's those that I want to address myself to now. For one thing, you'll almost always make a bad impression if you constantly fidget around in your chair as your boss is talking to you, or if you fail to look him in the eye, or if you clearly become evasive when you're talking. I'm assuming you're basically an honest, straightforward person, and it's important for you to *appear* that way if you're going to make a good impression.

Posture is another important factor. If you slouch while you're standing or sitting in a chair across from your boss, you'll reduce the impact of what you're trying to communicate. Some think there is an advantage in being tall, but I'm convinced that no matter what your height, you will always appear forceful and tall enough if you just stand up straight! Good posture communicates self-confidence, and self-confidence is a key component in a successful image.

Another key concept in the way you use your body in a business situation is courtesy. For example, if you sprawl all over your chair, you may in effect be telling your boss, "I don't really have too much respect for you, so there's no reason for me to show you any deference or formality in the way I hold myself."

The same kind of rudeness might be conveyed if you pile your research materials on your boss's desk when you walk into his office, rather than on an empty chair or table. Another quirk that is particularly annoying is to have a person "violate your space" during a conversation. In other words, the individual moves too close, say within six inches or so of your face, and forces you to back away. In most cases, men and women who do this aren't even aware of the image they are projecting. But unless they change this practice, they may alienate and irritate their fellow workers, or perhaps even become the secret butt of office jokes.

The whole point of evaluating your body language in the office is to be sure that you're not doing something that is interfering with your ability to communicate to your colleagues and fellow workers. If people are focusing on your dirty fingernails, unpolished shoes, body odor, or any other physical quirk instead of on your skills, you should take steps to remove that obstacle immediately. Otherwise, you may find your upward progress impeded for a rather insignificant reason.

This discussion of some of the elements in developing an achiever image in your company has obviously dealt to a large extent with your outward appearance—the way you look to others. But at the same time, in delving into proper reading habits, methods of communication, and organization techniques, we haven't limited ourselves to a consideration of merely superficial factors.

A genuine, positive image *always* has to be more than skin-deep or you'll quickly find you're getting the reputation of being only a "surface" person, one who may look good at first but who lacks substance and staying power. You have to have the right image to pave the way for your next step up the corporate ladder.

But to stay on that step when you reach it and to have the power to move even higher, you must also acquire reservoirs of inner strength and character. It's at this point that the real inner nature of people at the top begins to emerge. Now that we understand some of the things that can help project an executive image, let's go beneath the surface and explore some of those deeper qualities that are prerequisites to further advancement.

CHAPTER 9

NICE GUYS CAN FINISH FIRST!

Magazines, movies, and the electronic media are full of negative stereotypes of the business executive. Here are just a few that I've encountered, directly or second hand, over the past few years:

—"Most top-level executives have no heart. They had to trample all over people to reach their positions. . . ."

—"I know one guy who fired this widow with a big family right before Christmas. . . ."

—"You have to be a little ruthless—be willing to stab a friend in the back occasionally—if you're going to compete effectively for promotions. . . ."

—"Motivation of employees is a myth! The only way a boss can wring more work out of a subordinate is to threaten him with being fired or trick him with deceitful arguments about productivity. . . ."

—"You've always got to look out for 'old number one' first! The other guy can take care of himself. . . ."

—"Every successful person has to lie at one time or another. . . ."

—"Personal morality has no application to big business. . . ."

The list could go on and on, but you get the point. And I'm sure there really *are* people who have risen to the top while doing some of these things. I know myths don't spring up out of thin air, so I'm willing to concede there may well be some substance behind these stereotypes.

But I have to believe that whatever negative characteristics may exist, they are a minor exception rather than the rule in the executive office. I know hundreds of high-level executives personally, and though they may not be perfect, I have yet to meet the so-called stereotype. And in my opinion, being a conniving, hard-nosed bad guy just doesn't work! I believe anybody who demonstrates one or more of these negative qualities to any significant degree is almost certainly doomed to fall short of his ambitions.

What I'm getting at is this: You'll find, if you haven't already, that it pays for *anyone* interested in promotions to be a nice guy. Now let me show you what I mean with a few illustrations from actual incidents on the job.

Most bosses who are on their way to the upper levels of management in their companies learn early that treating people fairly, or even with compassion, produces better results than playing the bully or running roughshod over a worker's sensibilities. If you really do fire that poor widow on Christmas Eve or stab a few friends in the back, I would rate your chances for truly high-level advancement close to zero.

One of the main reasons that concern for the welfare of those under you is so important is *motivation.* You can't inspire people to do their best for you if they distrust or despise you. People are the best investment any company has, and they are the best insurance you can get for your future success—if you can get them to recognize you as a competent, honest, and compassionate leader who is worth following.

When the time for promotion comes around and two or three key people, including you, are in the running, one major question *your* bosses will ask is: "How well does he develop and motivate his staff?" If you come out ahead in this comparison, you're likely to move ahead.

Something that happened to me at the first Penney store I managed taught me a valuable lesson about this principle of motivation. I was new in this management position, and I was quite eager to have everything done just right. One department in particular concerned me because its appearance wasn't up to the standards I would have set for it. So I decided I'd try to bring that department back to where it should be.

The way I went about it was my first big mistake. After you are promoted and are in charge of supervising a department or job in which you excelled, there is an almost overwhelming temptation to return to that job when you see someone who reports to you falling short of your standards. Resist that temptation! The reason you were promoted was that you were above average. You can't expect everyone to demonstrate the same skills you acquired through extensive experience.

But I wasn't as experienced then as I thought I was. Instead of pointing out some of the problems and letting the department manager make the changes himself, I asked my wife, Verna, to join me at the store one evening after everyone had gone home, and we started doing some rearranging.

After Verna and I had finished, the display of merchandise was much more appealing, and I slept soundly that night with the inner assurance that my department manager would be overjoyed and grateful about what I had done for him. His reaction, though, was the exact opposite. He was embarrassed and humiliated. "I would have come in last night and helped you with this," he said. "If you had just asked me to do it, I would have done it."

I was upset with myself—not because this man had reacted negatively to my intervention, but because I had hurt him. This incident haunted me for a long time, for I knew I had inadvertently undermined this fellow's sense of self-worth. He had been doing the best work he could at a new job, and he was learning more every day. But my impatience and insensitivity had in effect said to him, "You're inadequate, friend. In fact, you're so inadequate, I'm going to have to push you aside and completely take over your job."

But even though I fell miserably short in this test of my management abilities, I learned a valuable lesson. I saw that if you want to motivate people, you have to recognize them as members of a team. You have to find ways to let them participate and get the credit for the good things that happen in your company—even the good things for which *you* may be primarily responsible.

One of the most common ways I've discovered for sharing the credit with those who report to me is in brainstorming sessions. In a typical freewheeling discussion in most companies, everybody throws out a certain number of thoughts and suggestions. A good boss will keep track of which idea came from which person, and then in his summary he'll compliment the various workers who made significant contributions. In fact, even if the boss had the most important role in shaping the final concept, I think it's a good idea for him to downplay his part and highlight what his subordinates have done. This is not dishonest—it's merely a way of passing psychological rewards around.

The previous chairman at JCPenney, who was my boss for a number of years, liked to cite a slogan that a general he had served under in the Army used to have on the wall behind his desk: "You can accomplish almost anything if you don't care who gets the credit." That thought has stuck with me, because I've learned in practice that it's really true.

This approach to motivation is a far cry from some of those tough stereotypes listed at the beginning of this chapter, wouldn't you say?

Of course, being a nice guy on the job doesn't mean that if you're a boss, you should slip into an ineffectual friendliness-at-any-price attitude. For a company to function properly, business and ethical standards must be maintained and corporate objectives achieved. To reach these goals, strict discipline may sometimes be in order, such as when a worker fails to perform properly on the job.

To put this point another way, compassion must always be tempered by justice. You may be genuinely touched by the personal problems of a person under you. But if you've been given the responsibility of supervising many people, you have to keep in mind the welfare of *everyone*—your entire business team—and not just the contentment or needs of one individual.

In administering discipline, it's a common practice and certainly quite wise to schedule a "corrective interview" at which you tell the individual exactly what he's doing wrong and what the consequences of his conduct may be if he doesn't change his ways. But sometimes, this kind of straight talking just isn't enough to resolve the problem.

Perhaps the person is a square peg in a round hole: He may be perfectly intelligent and diligent, but he has simply ended up in the wrong company or the wrong job. Or your employee may be lazy or a disruptive influence in the office. Whatever the difficulty, your responsibility as the supervisor may force you to take some unpleasant steps to correct the situation. You may even have to fire him.

I can still remember the first time I fired a person. Firing people is as hard for me now as it was then, but I think I've learned a few things about how to exercise discipline more effectively. That first time, as an assistant manager in a store, I found myself trying to get a reasonable amount of work out of a young man who was a classic goof-off. He was intelligent, but he wouldn't listen to instructions I gave him, and the result was periodic chaos in any department he touched.

I would tell him, "Okay, put ten-dollar labels on that entire group of shoes." But when I returned to check his work, I'd find he had priced them at one dollar—and they were going like hotcakes to customers who had discovered a real bargain!

Or I might tell him to put out some white shirts, and he would bring out striped shirts instead. Finally, about an hour before quitting time one day, his inattention and mistakes exasperated me so much I said sharply, "That's it! You're through! I want you to collect your pay and get your things out of here."

Apparently, my displeasure came through a little too clearly, because the young fellow decided to retaliate. He seemed to accept my decision at first, but after he had collected his pay and got ready to leave, he walked over to the old, manually operated elevator and sent it full-speed down to the basement. It crashed onto the big springs at the bottom, the cables unraveled, and the whole thing was out of service for three days. I was then in charge of supervising repairs and apologizing to disgruntled customers who were forced to use the stairs.

In retrospect, I know I should have handled this young man's discharge differently. For example, I should have terminated him at the very end of the day and then watched him closely until he left the building. He was clearly a volatile and immature type whom I should have expected to react erratically. If you think a person may respond angrily or even violently on being terminated, it's wise to take steps to protect company property and to ensure that the departure causes as little disruption as possible.

As part of any discussion of terminating people, however, it's important to note that the company often must bear much responsibility for the effectiveness of the individual in a particular job. After all, it's the company that did the screening, interviewing, hiring, and training. Companies that tend to have the lowest employee turnover rates and highest levels of individual performance usually do the best job of preliminary screening and have the best personal development programs. Also, companies that pay close attention to their hiring practices will lower their unemployment compensation insurance costs. The reason is that a person who is hired and trained properly is less apt to end up in an unemployment claims office.

Unfortunately, it's all too common to find an individual who has been kept on for a long time, well beyond his usefulness to the company. When the ax finally falls in such a situation, everyone involved suffers more than should have been necessary. For example, you might find a person who has been with an organization for ten years and during the entire time has received evaluations from a series of bosses who all had substantially the same thing to say: "This person is performing below our standards, and he must improve." But he *doesn't* improve, and nobody has done anything about the situation.

Perhaps some of the supervisors were reluctant to fire

him because he was such a nice person. Or perhaps none of the bosses had the stomach for a personal confrontation. In any case, circumstances almost always arise which force a decision to terminate the person. And if the company has in effect led him on by implying that he was doing a good enough job to retain his employment, the ultimate decision to terminate him could be much more painful than if it had been accomplished at an earlier date.

For example, the person might now be at an age when his children are in college and he has a more urgent need of a steady income stream. Or he may be approaching retirement and be unable to get a decent job any longer. In such a case, the person suffers more, and the company has lost far more than was warranted in "carrying" an unproductive worker for so long. In addition, your company could face some kind of discrimination suit.

In contrast to this sort of disaster, I've found it's often possible to discharge people in such a way that you can help them in their careers—and let them know you're helping them. There are several steps that are advisable to take before releasing a person, and the result is usually an employee who leaves with a good taste in his mouth and often even a good word to say to outsiders about his experience with the company. In my encounter with the stock boy, I can see now that if I had handled him in a firm yet more understanding way, he might not have felt a need to take out his frustrations on our elevator.

Occasionally, displeasure, frustration, or even anger about the inadequate work a person has been doing may cause you to want to fire him. Your feelings may build up and one final incident may cause you to blow your top. To guard against such an outburst, it's important to get control over your emotions before doing anything else about the situation. One effective method is a variation of the "count-to-ten-before-you-say-anything" technique. Here's how it works:

Sit back in your chair and go over all your encounters with the offending individual as objectively as you can. During these moments of reflection, try to step into the other person's shoes and ask, "How would *I* react to what I'm about to say?"

Many times, I find this period of private analysis helps me to tone down or completely eliminate some of the things I might originally have planned to mention. It's one thing to tell a person the truth about his bad performance, but quite another to use the truth as a verbal sledgehammer to punish and humiliate.

Also, the further you can remove yourself in time and emotion from the incident that has prompted you to discipline an employee, the more in control of yourself you'll find you become. If the back of your neck is still bristling or you're playing mental movies in your mind in which you verbally destroy the person, you know you're on dangerous ground.

The ultimate goal in letting an employee go should not be to tell him off. Instead, you should strive to part on the most amiable terms possible—and even help him in some positive way if you can. It's quite common for personnel experts in a company to help a discharged employee find another job that's more suitable to his interests and talents.

One common way to accomplish this in larger companies is to give the worker notice of his termination but then refer him to an "outplacement unit" in the personnel department. The specialists in this unit then direct their energies toward helping the employee find another position in another company that would suit his talents and interests better. Typically, this outplacement process involves interviewing the individual to assess his strong and weak points, helping him build a new résumé, coaching him in how to go through a job interview, and then working with him closely as he pursues his new job search.

Sometimes, though, it may seem more reasonable to offer to *demote* a person rather than fire him. There are a couple of reasons that this avenue may seem best. First of all, the company may have promoted the person faster than he was able to develop the skills needed for a new job. The potential and capacity to learn may be there, but it's just necessary to move back a few notches and go a little slower up the ladder. In many cases, the reason this procedure is necessary is that some supervisor has exercised poor judgment in deciding how fast a person should be promoted.

But secondly, it may be appropriate to offer to let a person continue with the company in a lower position because the Peter Principle has caught up with him—he has finally arrived at the level of his incompetence. This individual may have turned in a great performance at his last job, but he just can't hack it in the new position. So you may want to offer him an opportunity to return to his old job indefinitely.

Obviously, it takes a special kind of person to be able to take a demotion with equanimity and without rancor or resentment that may affect his morale and performance. But often this situation works out well, especially when you're dealing with a person who is quite conscious of job security and is worried about losing a good salary and benefits just prior to retirement.

Most executives I know who have moved to the upper management plateaus in their companies have been willing to spend time in counseling not only those who are being discharged or demoted, but also any other workers with personal problems. Taking time with employees this way tends to build loyalty and goodwill in them. Also, other employees see they are working for an understanding boss, and their morale and productivity are more likely to go up accordingly.

I know of one case in which a high executive learned one of his best staff people had a daughter who was suffering from a serious disease. The girl needed to live in a warm climate as part of her cure, but the office where these people were working was in a northern city. So the employee informed his boss he had to give his family's needs priority and look for a job elsewhere.

Instead of just accepting the man's resignation, though, the supervisor called him into his office several times for some personal counseling. They explored ways the person might stay in the company and yet still resolve his problem with the daughter's health—and a solution did finally emerge. The staff worker was transferred down to one of the company's branches in Southern California for a job with lesser responsibilities. But both he and the company officers understood there would be immediate opportunities for advancement if he continued to perform well.

Soon the worker began to prove his abilities in the new location. Before long, he had moved up to a management level well above where he had been before his transfer. His morale was high because his family difficulties had been corrected, and he was more inclined to work hard for a company with a supervisor who had been willing to work with him on his personal problem.

The best executive, then, is not a heartless executive. You always get better performances out of happy people, and the way to keep people happy is to treat them fairly, with a genuine attempt to understand their personal problems and concerns.

I know some people who would consistently encourage their subordinates to postpone vacations and work extra hours. Yet I've also learned from experience that this approach limits a person's effectiveness as a manager over the long haul. On many occasions, I've suggested to an employee, "Look, you've really been doing more than what's been expected. But maybe this is a good time for you and your family to think about vacation. I think the rest of us can keep things going for a couple of weeks while you're away."

Very few can take the strain of business pressure and overwork without a break, and it's up to you, as a manager on the way up the ladder, to become sensitive to the needs of your subordinates.

But what if you're on the other side of the fence, as the employee whose boss *isn't* very sensitive to your needs? Does it pay for you to be a nice guy in this situation?

Generally speaking, I think it's always best to avoid getting into a confrontation with your supervisor—especially in public. In business meetings I've occasionally seen the ranking officer or manager say something cutting or put a person down rather roughly. But it's advisable to avoid responding in kind. You might win a verbal battle by coming up with a quip that will temporarily give you an upper hand over one of your superiors. But you're almost always certain to lose the war, as you compete in the future for promotions.

It's usually best to approach the offending supervisor *after* the meeting and try to smooth things over. For example, you might say something like: "I must not have communicated very well yesterday, because I think what I was trying to say was important. If you have a couple of minutes, I'd like to explain in a little more detail what I was getting at."

If you can set up better lines of communication in

private like this, the chances are that your superior will treat you more respectfully in the next group session. In any case, I can't think of any circumstances in which I would choose to get into a public contest with my boss; I think I'd always be sure to lose in the long run.

Actually, if you can encourage your boss to communicate more sensitively in group meetings, you'll be helping *him* as well as yourself. The manager who gets a reputation for being cutting and abusive in business meetings usually finds fewer people being willing to contribute to the discussion. After all, who wants to suggest an idea if there's a good chance he'll be ridiculed? Young, inexperienced workers tend to be most affected by this threatening atmosphere, and the manager loses potentially helpful input from the more timid members of his staff.

There is one other important area in which false executive stereotypes have to be exposed, and that involves the question of *empire-building*.

Some people believe that to get ahead in most companies, you have to stake out a certain territory, gain dominance in that territory, and finally increase the size of your territory. ("Territory" in this context would generally be defined to include your staff, working budget, and areas of responsibility.) The result of getting a "big" empire, popular wisdom says, is that you'll strengthen your position to take the next step up in the corporate hierarchy.

Unfortunately, such empire-building is counterproductive for the company—and productivity is a major consideration in promotions these days so this approach may do much more harm than good to a person's efforts to advance in a company. Let me give you an illustration from the "Hay point" system, a common but rather complex method for setting corporate pay scales.

The concept of the Hay point was originated by the Hay Associates personnel consulting firm to help big corporations establish equitable and competitive pay practices for widely divergent occupational positions. There are, by the way, a number of other, similar pay-rating systems that a company may employ, such as a T.P.F. & C. system (Towers, Parents, Foster & Crosby) that we use at JCPenney.

Now, here's an illustration of how one of the point systems may work. It may seem hard to relate the jobs of auditor, factory foreman, and distribution supervisor for pay purposes in a company. But if you can assign each job a certain range of points and then pay workers according to the points assigned to them, you can greatly simplify your pay-scale problems.

A basic principle is that the number of points assigned to your job determines how high your salary will be. Generally, every job level carries with it a minimum and maximum number of points, so that people with the same title and seemingly the same job may be compensated at different salaries. Also, the point ranges tend to overlap from one level to the next, so that a person with a lower title may actually be getting paid more than a person with a higher title.

For example, you might be holding down a job that can be compensated with a salary of $30,000 to $38,000, and the job of the person just above you may have a pay range of $35,000 to $43,000. As a result, you can see it's possible for you to move to the upper range of your pay scale and at some point actually be earning more than a person who has a title higher than yours, but who is at the lower end of his pay scale.

I'm on the board at Citibank, which uses the Hay point system. Executives on their way up in the company are quite aware of the significance of the number of Hay points assigned to them. I can remember a tennis match I was playing with the chairman of Citicorp/Citibank and a couple of his younger executives. The game was quite close, and in the midst of the banter back and forth, the Citicorp chief jokingly called out, "I don't want to influence how you're playing this game, but I should point out that Mr. Seibert is on the Personnel Committee and is in a position to influence your Hay points!"

Of course, everyone knew I wasn't about to try to influence anyone's Hay points. But unfortunately there is a temptation for some employees to try to manipulate any system to their personal advantage. The guidelines for moving up in point ranges in different positions vary from company to company. But generally speaking, factors like seniority, number of staff members reporting to you, and size of your office budget may help determine your pay rating.

Some workers might thus be tempted to think, "If I can convince my boss to let me hire two more people and increase the budget for my projects by another $100,000, I could get a considerable increase in pay through more points, and I might even be up for promotion sooner!"

The danger in this kind of thinking is that a manager may become preoccupied with improving his pay rating and artificially creating a bigger job for himself. Even if this ploy works at first and you do get a little more money, you still have to justify the need you've expressed for a larger staff or a bigger budget. As a result, if you were merely attempting to pad your "empire" to help yourself and not the company, your scheme would probably ultimately become apparent and you would be in considerably worse shape than you were in before you embarked on this path.

Each individual is evaluated over the long haul by the way he has performed his assigned job at a given level of responsibility. Nobody will care five years from now what your Hay points were today. But they *will* care about how you improved company profits or executed your responsibilities.

So I would advise you very strongly not to worry about beating the system—whether it's Hay points, or the T.P.F. & C. system, or some other pay scale. Instead, concentrate on doing your job well and following the other basic principles we've discussed in expediting your movement toward the top. If you try to develop into a good person and a good leader, you'll find you don't need to worry about beating any system or manipulating some situation. Instead, the various institutional structures and programs in your company will tend to work in your favor automatically. And you'll discover that nice guys really *can* finish first.

CHAPTER 10

The PROMOTION PRINCIPLE:

Self-Appraisal, Personal Productivity, Choosing a Mentor

Everything you do on the job has some bearing on your ability to be promoted. In fact, this entire book is designed to teach you as much as I know about the promotion process in business. So you may ask, "What's the point in devoting a special chapter to this topic?"

The reason this discussion is important is that I believe there are several key factors which constitute a "promotion principle"—a principle that can help give the final shove to open that door to the next management level in your company. Everything we've discussed so far has enabled you to move up *to* that door. But somehow, you've got to make it swing open. In a way, this process reminds me of the salesman who is able to introduce his product and prime his buyer, but who still must take that final step of closing the sale.

There are several main elements which make up the promotion principle, including three that I want to spend some time discussing at this point—the individual appraisal process, the development of a high level of personal productivity, and the role of mentors in a person's upward movement in a corporation.

1. The appraisal process.

After a certain point, no matter where you are in the company hierarchy, you'll have to fall back on your own resources and learn how to appraise your own standing and skills in relation to your competitors.

For example, how does the quality of your work stand up to that of your peers? How do you look in the eyes of your boss? What ways can you improve upon your performance? How will your work stack up in the next appraisal interview that's conducted by your boss?

Developing a sense of detachment about your accomplishments so that you can evaluate yourself objectively and then take the necessary steps to do a better job is certainly a key element in what we've described as the promotion principle. To understand this concept, I'm going to ask you to take out a pencil and a few sheets of paper and then do some writing about yourself.

First, put the title "Objectives" at the top of one sheet of paper. Then, write "Business Strengths" at the top of the second sheet. Finally, jot down "Business Weaknesses" at the top of the third sheet.

Now, under "Objectives," list the goals you hope to achieve while working in your *present* position. Remember: Our focus in this book has been living by the day and concentrating on the tasks at hand—not on some business "pie in the sky" far off in the future.

Next, spend a few minutes thinking about both your strengths and weaknesses on your current job. It's probably easiest to do these two lists at the same time, because remembering a certain strength may trigger the thought of a corresponding weakness.

After you've completed these lists, sit back and spend a few minutes thinking about what you can do to achieve the objectives you've put down, how you can use your strengths, and how you can overcome or minimize your weaknesses. Relate each of these characteristics to your present job. Then, begin to formulate a strategy in your mind for using your strong points as a foundation to move even more forcefully toward the goals you've set for yourself.

Now, jot down the conclusions and strategies you've come to, and save these papers to use as a basis for evaluating your progress. You should go through this exercise at least once a year to be sure you know exactly where you're going and how you hope to get there.

This series of exercises can help you understand more about your inner self—your goals in life and your potential for achieving them. But it's also important to evaluate yourself in relation to your colleagues, with whom you're competing for promotion to the next management level in your business. This second part of your self-appraisal should also be done on a piece of paper so that you can get a clear-cut picture, in black and white, of your precise situation.

Entitle this sheet "Team Members." Now, list the people on your level who may be in the running for higher-level jobs that you yourself would like. Beside each name, make a few notes about the major strengths and weaknesses of the person and indicate how you think you compare with him or her.

I'm not trying to inspire an unhealthy kind of competition between you and your peers, nor am I attempting to lay the basis for you to increase your envy level. I'm just encouraging you to be realistic and increase your opportunities to improve yourself. If you know one of your colleagues is far superior to you in aptitude and education in one field, such as computer applications, perhaps you should do some extra study to bring yourself up to par in this area. Or if there is an alternative route to promotion that you can take by relying on some ability where you are stronger, maybe you should take that path. The main idea here is to learn where you stand in relation to others so that you can plan a career strategy that has the best chance for success.

You'll note that all this talk about "strategy" in your career is focused on the job at hand—not on some position several levels up in the company. All your thoughts and efforts should center on ways to improve yourself and excel *in the present*, not in the future. The future will take care of itself if you'll just take the pains to build a firm foundation right now.

The third and final step in this self-appraisal process is to evaluate yourself in light of your relationships with your superiors, and especially your immediate boss. Again, take out a sheet of paper and label it "Boss." Now think: Do you communicate well with him? Is it easy to talk with him, or do you often feel uncomfortable in his presence? List all the good and bad features of this relationship, and then sit back and study them. Star the two most important deficiencies in your contacts with your supervisor and try to come up with a plan to improve your relationship in those areas.

This last step in appraising yourself can be especially useful if your company periodically provides you with appraisal interviews from your boss on your progress. This interview won't do you any good at all if you and your supervisor can't talk openly with each other. So it's helpful to lay the groundwork for a formal appraisal interview by trying to stimulate as many *informal* appraisal meetings as possible at other points during the year.

For you to get the most out of a meeting like this with

your boss, it's essential that he feel free to tell you exactly what he thinks about how you've been doing. But put yourself in his shoes. If a person under you has been doing a bad job in some area, it may be hard to criticize or reprimand. It's much easier to dwell on the good parts of his performance and skim over the negative things. The negatives are still there, though, and they are likely to get worse if an employee is not notified about them. So let your boss know you appreciate constructive criticism—primarily because you know you're not perfect and you want to turn your weaknesses into strengths.

Finally, let me reemphasize one point I made earlier: You lose many of the benefits of making these lists and going through a self-appraisal process if you just throw the lists away or lose them. Put them in a permanent file in your home and get into the habit of adding regularly to that file and consulting it to get some idea of the progress you're making. You'll be surprised at how much better you can get to know yourself—and improve your business abilities—just by going through these simple, short exercises periodically.

2. Personal productivity.

Productivity, or the ability to increase the efficiency and output of the staff assigned to you, is perhaps the key concern in the nation's corporations these days. But one of the misconceptions about productivity is that it is often considered the result of making people work harder or put out more. That may happen, but it's only one element in the concept. Generally, the way that you make people more productive personally relates only in part to motivation or to getting people to work harder.

More likely, though, productivity will depend on coming up with better ways to get the job done—or in business parlance, improving your "systems."

Better communications skills, production concepts, and goal setting are key factors here. For example, automating statistical reports and thus eliminating the need for someone to punch up numbers on an adding machine or write them down in columns would greatly increase the output of a group of clerical people. Or installing word-processing machines rather than ordinary typewriters could improve productivity in certain offices by 20 to 50 percent.

Or take the task employees in many businesses have of managing an inventory: If you can get a computer system to speed up the process of analysis of inventory items and provide instant information that otherwise would have to be computed by hand, your operation will become more efficient and productive.

Also, you can become more productive if you can come up with better ways to use physical assets under your supervision. For example, more efficient use of any space you're renting may save you money, help increase your output, and thereby contribute to productivity. Furthermore, if you are in charge of energy used in your plant or office, such as electricity and heating fuels, there are probably many ways to save money in this area. Perhaps you also have money that can be used more efficiently: For instance, unnecessary cash on hand is unproductive and should be looked at in terms of the best investment opportunities.

So there are many ways to increase productivity without just trying to get people to work harder. Of course, I can't get too specific in giving you advice about increasing your output, because productivity is a very personal thing which must be defined differently from job to job and company to company. But as a general rule, improving your productivity is certainly something to concentrate on, because the highly productive person is in a very strong position in terms of future promotions. He is the one who will probably be selected to take the leadership in training others in the company how to become more productive. And that's the kind of person that everyone wants to see move up to the higher echelons on the corporate ladder.

3. The mentor.

Much has been written lately about the importance of having one or more mentors in the climb up the corporate ladder. In my opinion, a mentor isn't really an essential element in a person's upward movement in business, but a mentor certainly can provide an additional positive dimension in the promotion process.

A mentor, or "rabbi" as some people call him, is a successful and relatively senior manager or executive who can advise and guide a younger person up the corporate ladder. According to a study in the *Harvard Business Review* by Gerald Roche, president of the Chicago management consulting firm of Heidrick & Struggles Inc., a mentor can occupy an important position in an individual's personal success scenario.

Roche, in surveying more than a thousand individuals holding jobs as senior vice-president and higher, found that 64 percent had enjoyed the assistance of mentors. About 33 percent of those responding said their mentor was the chief executive officer. Male executives averaged two mentors during their careers, and female executives averaged three. The study revealed that 70 percent of the mentors who helped the women executives were male.

The function of a mentor is to help you become a more efficient manager and to teach you practical techniques and information you haven't acquired through the ordinary learning process in your work. But I would not advise you to try to befriend a senior executive for the purely political purpose of having him pull some strings to get you promoted more quickly. Often this approach backfires, because most people who have made it to the top levels of a company pride themselves on being fair and evenhanded. If you try to encourage your mentor to show you favoritism, you may find he starts bending over backward *not* to give you any special breaks.

Establishing a relationship with a mentor, then, is not just a form of sophisticated, high-level apple-polishing. But you can get invaluable advice and guidance for your career if you recognize that you don't know everything and that you can learn from the senior officer who has offered a special hand of friendship.

There are also some other limits to this relationship. The best kind of mentor won't try to call the shots of your career on a daily basis. Instead, he will convey to you some of the principles he has learned over the years and help you begin to gain a storehouse of wisdom that will enable you to think and perform like executives who are many years your senior.

I've had several mentors during my career, and they've each inspired me to reach beyond what I thought were the limits of my abilities. They helped to open my mind to the idea that I might be able to achieve more in business than I originally thought I could.

For example, when I was a department manager in one store, one of my superiors took a special interest in me and pushed me to do better work whenever he got the chance. We were working together long hours on one project, and I thought I had been doing a good job—

perhaps even an outstanding job. But this particular mentor wouldn't let me drift off into complacency.

"Don, you may think you're working hard, but you're still not working up to your full capacity," he said. "We've got to finish this thing by the end of this week, and you're not going to complete your end of it unless you either get more efficient or put in more time."

I knew he was right, and so I started concentrating harder—and the job got done on time. He had challenged me to reach beyond myself, and as a result, I accomplished far more than I thought I could. On this and other occasions, this particular senior manager caused me to review my use of time and my capacity for hard work. The habits he instilled stuck with me long after I had moved on to another job in the company.

It's important to recognize here, though, that any mentor relationship probably won't be a permanent thing. You or your mentor could be transferred to another department or part of the country. If this happens, you shouldn't feel distressed or upset because this senior adviser is no longer available. It's virtually inevitable that *every* mentor will pass out of your life at some point in your career.

Also, there are times when what you're learning from a mentor is oriented more toward technical matters than management skills. In such a case, you may become more proficient than your teacher, and as you might expect, that sort of development will also end a relationship.

One of the best examples of this principle in my own life occurred when I was a high school student taking clarinet lessons. My teacher at one point was a general-purpose musician who taught a number of instruments to beginners and intermediates. After about two years of

instruction under him, I came to respect him as a professional and to like him very much just as a friend. So I
was shocked when he said one day, "I don't want to
teach you anymore, Don."

"Why not?" I asked, crestfallen and afraid I had done
something to offend him.

"I've taken you as far as I can," he replied. "You're a
better clarinetist now than I am, and you can become
much better. But you need a better teacher to get there."

He then recommended some other instructors, and I
began to look into them as potential teachers. Actually, I
still wanted to stay on with my old teacher, but I recognized finally that he was behaving in a responsible,
honest, mature way toward me. He was actually doing
me a big favor, and I learned to appreciate it more and
more as I got older and saw how the mentor relationship
worked in other situations.

It would be nice if every adviser and mentor you have
would take the same approach my clarinet teacher did,
but unfortunately you can't always expect that kind of
sensitivity in your business career. As a practical matter,
you will probably have to judge for yourself whether
you've outgrown your present adviser. If you decide you
have maintained the mentor relationship as long as
necessary, that doesn't mean, of course, that you can't
remain friends with your mentor. It just means that if
you want to get practical advice and instruction on how
to direct your career in the future, you will have to find a
more appropriate mentor.

But in all this discussion about mentors, it's important
to remember that you don't have to sit down for a series
of formal meetings each week or month with a particular
person for that person to qualify as a mentor. As a matter
of fact, the nature of your meetings with this person may

be quite informal. For example, they may take the form of occasional meetings in the company cafeteria or riding home with him on the train.

Generally speaking, then, I believe that a mentor is a person who (1) is more seasoned than you in an overall management sense or in a particular field of technical expertise, (2) takes a personal interest in your future, and (3) is willing to spend some time with you in a non-business kind of way to give his opinions and advice.

The *amount* of time you spend with a mentor is not necessarily of overriding importance, either. Perhaps you meet your mentor for a specific business discussion, and at the end of that session for about five or ten minutes, you engage in philosophical discussion or speculation about your career. If you find somebody giving you pointers or occasionally sharing with you a philosophy of management that you haven't solicited, you should recognize him as a person who is interested in your future—and as a potential mentor.

Of course, he may not have consciously selected you to serve as your mentor. But he may see enough promise in your future that from time to time he'll be willing to feed you things from his "memory banks" that you ought to know. And you should be sensitive enough to this sort of overture to pay attention.

An important part of the mentor relationship is that your mentor probably just likes you and perhaps sees you as a younger sibling in a sense. In most cases, the senior person will make the first approach in establishing this sort of relationship. But the junior person must be sensitive enough to know when the time has come to respond and be available for the informal training and support that is being offered.

So these three factors—self-appraisal, productivity, and mentors—are a significant part of what we've called the "promotion principle," or the group of factors which can usher you through various doors to higher positions in your company. But as you move into higher levels in your company, there are three additional factors which become increasingly dominant and important. I like to think of these as the final three rungs on the corporate ladder:

First, you have to streamline your personal decision-making processes. Next, you have to concentrate harder on being totally efficient in your use of the limited time available to you. Finally, you should be prepared to take risks in order to be in a position to compete for the very top positions in your company.

CHAPTER 11

BASIC STEPS *for* DECISION-MAKING

One of the first qualities corporate officers look for in a top-level executive is the ability to make decisions swiftly and efficiently. A capacity to make the right decision—whether under great pressure or not—can contribute to your reputation as a person of good judgment. And good judgment is an absolutely essential characteristic for a senior executive in any major corporation.

You may object, "My problem is that I'm naturally indecisive!" Or, "I always see several sides to a question. It's hard for me to make up my mind about going one way or another without taking a lot of time and attaching all sorts of qualifications."

I think we all face hesitations and reservations like these at various points in our lives. But no matter where you now stand as a decision-maker, you can improve your ability by learning some basic rules of the game and then working at developing certain skills that will enable you to play well under those rules. As we've already seen, many decisions aren't insulated or purely individual; they involve teamwork with several people contributing to the final decision. But there are also many times when one individual must make some final judgment, and the ability to play this "buck-stops-here" role requires certain special skills.

To help you improve your ability to make sound decisions on the job, let me first summarize the fundamentals of effective decision-making. Of course, top-level decision-making can get incredibly complex and sophisticated, with concepts like "decision trees," PERT networks, and various computer models. But to start you off, here are four basic steps:

Step 1: Define the question. In other words, be sure you understand the exact problem that you must resolve.

Step 2: List all possible answers to the question.

Step 3: Identify the risks and rewards connected with each possible answer. Put down all the pros and cons, with pluses and minuses, as you compare one route with another.

Step 4: Decide!

Throughout this process, seek advice and information which will help you arrive at the best answer.

At first glance, these four steps may seem rather abstract. But they have highly practical implications for all business decisions that confront you, from the simplest to the most complex. Let's first take a look at a rather simple decision that might have to be made in a typical retail store, just to illustrate how the process works.

Assume you're in charge of a department store in a city that has been put on a blizzard alert. The snow has already started to fall, and you have to decide whether and when to close your doors.

Now let me say at the outset that this is not a typical decision in a number of ways. For one thing, most important decisions would allow you much more time— perhaps as much as six months—for research and gathering information to give you the basis for making the final judgment. You would normally have to know the deadline by which the decision must be made, and you would schedule your information-gathering so that you could render your judgment in time to meet the deadline.

A major problem in productivity in many companies is that people who have to make decisions don't make them on time, and so a "slippage" in decision-making may occur. In other words, research and reports on decisions begin to pile up, past scheduled deadlines. As a result, bottlenecks in decision-making and reductions in the ability to take action may slow down the forward progress of the company's operations.

But even though this example of a blizzard we're about to examine isn't necessarily typical, it can still illustrate the general process of decision-making. So now consider what you might do when that initial weather forecast comes to your attention.

You would probably first want to assign someone to check several weather reports to see what the outlook is expected to be during the next few hours. Then, when you learn what the likeliest course of the storm will be, you would want to evaluate the transportation situation of your employees.

One of the first questions to ask would be: "By what time should we close to enable them to get home safely?" You would also want to check to see what the competition in town is doing. If you close your doors before everyone else does, you're going to lose some business. But if you're the only one left open, your workers may get resentful and wonder if you're trying to wring the last drop of blood out of them.

By now, as your information starts to come in, you can frame the basic question you need to ask. It might go something like this: "How long can I keep my store's doors open to offer sufficient competition to other merchants, and yet still allow my employees enough time to get home conveniently and safely?"

Some questions can be answered with a yes or no, but others, like this one, may have multiple answers. But as more information becomes available, even the most complex multiple-choice questions may answer themselves. You may find, for example, that all your competitor stores have already closed, and the storm is coming in so fast that your employees should leave immediately if they're going to get home at all. The answer in this case is simple: Close the store right now!

But if the facts are not that clear-cut, you have to outline the various possible solutions open to you and the rewards and risks connected with each. For example, half of your competitors may still be operating and you don't know when they plan to close. Also, you may have three conflicting weather reports, so you don't know the exact implications for your employees of staying open for another hour, or two hours, or three hours.

The contradictory information you're getting may seem confusing at first, but if you attack the problem systematically, an answer that is preferable to all others is bound to emerge. For example, you may discover that your business has dropped off noticeably as the blizzard approaches, and your employees are standing around more than they are selling to customers. In that case, it becomes more reasonable to close down and let your people go home: The risk of inconveniencing them begins to outweigh the potential rewards of additional sales. If business is booming even as the snow piles up outside, you might still want to close down because the safe transportation of your workers may have become a real factor.

After you have enough information and have outlined and analyzed your possible courses of action, you'll find many decisions that seemed tough at first are actually obvious and easy to answer. But there will still be occasional times when there seems to be only a nerve-racking 60 percent chance you'll succeed if you take one route—and, of course, a rather disturbing 40 percent chance you'll fail.

This relatively large risk of failure is enough to be of concern, especially if the risk may involve considerable amounts of company money or applications of manpower. But when you have the facts and analyses before you, you have to *force* yourself to act if you can't get motivated any other way. That's why step 4—"Decide!"—is so important. Some people are so afraid of making the wrong move that they become paralyzed, or they avoid making the obvious decision by returning to the drawing board and asking for more facts and more analyses.

Don't let this happen to you! There always comes a point at which you have to say, "That's it! I've done all I can do, given the time limitations and general uncertainties involved with this decision. Now, I have to act." If you fail to take this last step, you'll get the reputation of being indecisive when tough decisions confront you, and that sort of image can be damaging to your efforts to maintain your upward progress in the company.

As chief executive officer of JCPenney, for example, I've found myself involved in both simple and highly complex decisions that relate to the company's total public image. But even though I may be dealing with issues that have a potentially broader impact than those in the lower levels of management, the basic decision-making process remains the same.

For example, we have been faced with the need at different times to deemphasize or withdraw from parts of our operations. Generally, strategic or financial considerations were resolved primarily on merit, on what we believed would provide the company with the highest level of profit and at the same time give the public the best deal possible. But the decision-making process also involved a consideration of the effect on our own associates in those operations, the reaction of the financial community, the effect on customer attitudes toward us, and the assessment of our actions by our stockholders. These elements, plus the complexity of implementing a new approach to our operations, have presented us with extremely difficult decisions.

But even challenging decisions relating to matters like these have been subjected to the same basically simple decision-making process described above, with results that were generally given good marks by all the affected or interested parties. Of course, you never can satisfy everyone, especially when the issues are complex and the results touch many people.

In making many decisions, you're certain to make some mistakes. But as long as you follow the steps that have been outlined and do a reasonable job of collecting your facts and analyzing them, you'll make the right choice most of the time. The more experience you get in this decision-making process, the more proficient you'll become. When I face a tough, hard-to-call decision, I find some comfort from these words of managment expert Peter Drucker: "A decision is a judgment. It is a choice between alternatives. It is rarely a choice between 'almost right' and 'probably wrong.'"

But effective decision-making is only one of several skills or qualities you must acquire if you hope to move up to the highest levels of management. Another important factor is the expertise you show in managing your time as you carry out your executive duties.

CHAPTER 12

The EXECUTIVE TIME CRUNCH

"There are simply not enough hours in the day to do what I want to do!"

Most people make this complaint at one time or another, but senior executives face such packed schedules that they may feel like muttering these words every minute of every day.

As you move toward higher levels in your company, you'll find this time problem intensifies to the point that you can no longer think about your time in the normal way. In effect, you enter a new dimension of time management which forces you to take a completely different approach to ordering your day and accomplishing your tasks.

In the midst of this time crunch, it may sometimes seem there are not enough days in the week to accomplish what you're expected to do in just one morning. If you take the wrong approach to carrying out your responsibilities, you may find yourself living through ongoing anxiety attacks—and the stress you'll undergo won't help your health or your efficiency one whit. All executives may experience the feeling of being completely overwhelmed at some point, but there are ways to minimize the sense of anxiety and frustration.

Here are eight techniques I've picked up over the

years which enable me—as well as many other executives—to operate more effectively in what might be called "executive time management":

• **Prepare a raw-time budget.** If you're having trouble getting control of all your responsibilities, this is the first step to take to get back on the right track. Over a period of one week, note on a pad of paper exactly how you spend your hours on the job.

Include coffee breaks, lunches, and informal conversations about yesterday's sports contests, as well as time spent behind the desk and at formal business meetings. Also, don't forget your commuting time. If you're often away on trips, you might detail a typical week on the road, with similar notations about the way you spent your working hours.

After you've collected these data, sit down with another piece of paper and list each category of activity, with an indication of the total amount of time you actually spent on the activity during the week. Now you should have a fairly good picture of how you spend a typical week. Some ideas are probably already dawning as to how much time you're wasting and what steps you may be able to take to adjust the allocation of the limited numbers of hours in your weekly schedule.

In analyzing my own schedule, I've learned that I spend about 70 percent of my time while I'm at the New York City offices in meetings, and the other 30 percent in desk work. But my commitments tend to vary considerably from one week to the next, because I frequently have to attend dinners, give speeches, or go to meetings in other cities or locations.

But I still find it very important to keep close track of where my hours are going each day in order to maintain some degree of efficiency in my use of time. For example, I've learned that I need to set aside a half day *before I leave* on a trip to complete unfinished business and plan the final details of my travel schedule. Otherwise I'll find myself facing a host of loose ends when I return to the office.

Also, it's important for me to allocate sufficient time at the beginning of the week, and preferably an entire Monday, *after I return* from a trip so that I can dispose of the mail and other business that has come into my office while I've been gone. If I don't make this time available, it becomes difficult to catch up while handling current work, and before I know it, I'm off on another trip and in danger of getting further behind.

 • **Remember that the higher you go, the more you must let go.** This is one of the key principles that should guide you as you approach executive management of time. At the lower management levels, you may have a fairly large number of people working for you, but you don't have access to the depth of staff support that accompanies higher positions. At the top levels of a big corporation, much of the routine work can and should be done by somebody other than the executive. And the obvious way to shift this work to others is to delegate.

It's important, though, to distinguish between effective delegation and imposing "make-work" projects on your subordinates. Delegation should always involve work which *has* to get done—work which *you* will end up doing if one of your employees doesn't. You obviously can't do all the work under your supervision in your company, and the more you can spread around to others, the more time you'll find you have to come up with new concepts to make the entire operation more productive.

You may find you're working under an executive who isn't very good at delegation and, in fact, is wasting your time by piling unnecessary work on you or by keeping you in his office too often. In such a case, you might try communicating the problem to him by presenting him with a variation on the raw-time budget.

Just keep track of how you're spending your hours on the job for a week or so, and be sure to include the amount of time you're spending in his office: If it's seven hours a week, enter that on your time analysis. Then go in to him, explain that you're feeling pressed with your work, and show him the time log you've kept. You might ask, "Do you see any way I could become more efficient?"

If he bothers to read the time analysis you've written on yourself, he's bound to get the point that he's using too much of your time. And you'll be likely to find that you have most of those hours free in the future for your other tasks. Also, you may have given your superior a gentle lesson in what constitutes delegation and what involves a mere wasting of a worker's time.

• **Learn to organize your correspondence.** There are two basic steps in handling your correspondence efficiently—establishing a workable intake system, and delegating as much correspondence as possible to others. The system I've set up is to use one large drawer in my desk for all incoming correspondence. This has to serve as my "in basket," because no ordinary basket would be large enough to contain the amount of mail I get. I have five folders in the drawer, one for each working day.

While I'm out of town or away from my office at meetings for a day or so, my secretary will deposit all my Monday mail in the Monday folder. The Tuesday mail will be placed in the Tuesday folder, and so on. Then, when I return to the office, I'll first go through the earliest mail which came in, then the next day's mail, and then the next until I finally bring myself up to date.

As I said before, I set aside as much time as necessary on the Monday I return from a trip to go through my mail. I usually start early in the morning and keep going until I make the progress that I feel is necessary. I'll put every piece on the top of my desk and sort it into piles that I can delegate to others, and other piles I have to do myself.

The materials that can be delegated are immediately assigned an office reference slip, and they are forwarded to the person who has been chosen to handle them. As for the matters I've elected to dispose of myself, I make sure that when I'm traveling or waiting for a meeting to get started, I have them in my possession. Then, when a spare moment comes along, I pull out a small recorder I carry around with me and dictate answers to the pending correspondence.

I think anybody can learn to get on top of his correspondence if he'll just be systematic and refuse to allow himself to put off working on it. Once you say, "I don't feel like doing my mail this morning—I think I'll try something else instead," you're well on your way to being overwhelmed. You may never look forward to large accumulations of mail, but an organized approach will reduce it to manageable work.

• **Practice "early bird" decision-making.** Many people waste a great deal of time mulling over essentially the same decision on several different occasions.

For example, you may be invited to attend or participate in professional seminars or other outside meetings. Instead of having to ponder your involvement in each of these events, you might be able to determine in advance that there are certain times of the year, perhaps because of a heavy office workload, when you won't be able to attend any outside functions. As a result, you can just inform your secretary to turn down the invitations automatically during your heavy seasons; that way, you won't have to devote any time to considering each individual event.

I've also found that it's often possible to sit down with my staff and work out guidelines for certain speaking engagements and other public responsibilities well in advance of any invitations. If you use a similar approach and think through your own personal priorities before you confront various requests and invitations, you'll already have a standing policy for how to handle many demands on your time. Then all you'll have to do is say yes or no, without being forced to deliberate in detail over everything that crosses your desk.

• **Learn how to keep lists.** Efficient people at all levels of management are accomplished list-keepers, and this practice is particularly imperative during those periods when you are unusually pressed for time.

A good way to use lists is to take time at the end of a day or the first thing in the morning and write down what you want to accomplish during the upcoming workday. You might list fifteen things you want to do. Then go over the list carefully and set up priorities— what you want to do first, second, third, and so on down the line.

Don't expect to finish up every item on your list each day. Usually, that would be an impossibility. Instead, do the most important things and then carry the others over to the next day. Unfinished jobs stay on the list until they get accomplished or until it becomes obvious there is no need to do them at all.

It's essential, though, that you learn where to draw the

line in your list-making. Lists should be a tool, not an obsession. I have known people who try to organize their time weeks in advance, but this is usually a complete waste of time.

• **Postpone interesting tasks.** Occasionally I find there are some jobs I'm not getting done, no matter how often I put them down on my daily things-to-do lists. In this case, I know the tasks I'm putting off are basically distasteful to me for some reason, and that's a signal that the time has come for me to grit my teeth and do them, whether I like it or not.

One way I've found to be sure I finish certain jobs I may not like is to make a conscious decision to postpone the jobs and activities that I find particularly interesting. I know, as a practical matter, I'm eventually going to do those things I really like to do—even if I have to do them at home. So I schedule the unpleasant jobs early in the morning, get them out of the way, and put myself in a position to enjoy the remainder of the day that much more.

• **Turn your secretary into your supervisor.** Don't get me wrong! I'm not suggesting you turn over your management duties to your secretary. But I am saying you should set up your schedule and office procedures and then put him or her in charge of helping you adhere to them.

The higher you go in the company, the more important your personal secretary becomes. The best secretaries are those who not only have the basic typing, filing, and office-management skills, but also have the intelligence and sensitivity to understand how their bosses think. This latter quality is absolutely essential if your secretary is going to be able to help you save time in screening calls and correspondence.

I could spend at least fifteen minutes a day just throwing junk mail into the wastebasket if my secretary didn't know which things I would automatically get rid of and which I would feel should get more attention. And if I'm in an important meeting which requires that my telephone calls be held, she knows there are exceptions that may require me to be interrupted. For example, a call from the chairman of the Business Roundtable always goes through to me because I know he will likely have something important to say.

So I would advise you to select your secretary with extreme care and devote some time to discussing with him or her exactly what your objectives are in every phase of your work. A secretary who understands the reasons behind the procedures you set up will be much more likely to make the right decision when something out of the ordinary comes into the office.

• **Rely on your inner resources.** The pressures and frustrations of business management can get you down at times unless you learn to put things in perspective. And this means learning to shift your intellectual and emotional gears by viewing your work in the context of your personal value system, which we discussed earlier in this book.

At those times when my workload seems overwhelming, I take a short break to put things into perspective. These times of reflection generally result in changing the "overwhelming" into the "manageable."

Another way of gaining perspective on a situation through your inner resources is to fall back on your sense of humor. Almost every serious crisis has a tinge of humor about it, and if you can just find that amusing element and focus on in for a few moments, you'll probably find yourself relaxing more almost immediately. In this case, it's not a matter of laughing off or taking lightly a weighty responsibility. Rather, it's a question of finding a way to release pent-up tensions and anxieties that may be immobilizing you and preventing you from doing your best.

In my opinion, any technique you can find to help you detach yourself from your surroundings and pressures can be tremendously beneficial in providing additional flexibility in dealing with serious problems. Many times, when I have had my nose to the grindstone for too long, I may *seem* to be making some progress. But actually, I may be restricting my vision and missing a technique or method that would make me much more creative and efficient.

In this chapter and the previous one, we've examined two important steps which can smooth the way in your movement to the upper levels of corporate management. First we saw how a good manager should go about making decisions; then we looked at ways an executive can overcome the increasing crunch on his time.

Now we're ready to explore the final rung on the business ladder—the personal characteristics that may be found in those who have made it to the very top of their companies.

CHAPTER 13
The TOP of the LADDER

"It's lonely at the top!"

"The buck stops here."

"The lives of the many are controlled by the few."

"Stop crime in the suites!"

These and other clichés have been applied at one time or another to the chief executive officers of major corporations and have contributed to an executive mystique that makes many people wonder, "Exactly what does it take to be able to move up that very last step, to the top rung of the corporate ladder? Are those few CEOs in the nation's corporate suites a completely different breed of human being?"

In the attempt to answer these questions, a variety of myths—some of them rather negative—have sprung up. For one thing, CEOs often meet together socially or in business action groups like the Business Roundtable. In some people's minds this camaraderie has led to a suspicion that the main goal of top people in the biggest corporations is somehow to develop arcane capitalistic devices as a way to control the lives of ordinary citizens. Sometimes there is even a tendency to believe in a kind of dark conspiracy among these supposedly mean-spirited high-level executives.

This attitude may be best expressed by the essayist Frank Moore Colby, who wrote earlier in this century, "I have found some of the best reasons I ever had for remaining at the bottom simply by looking at the men at the top."

These ideas are foreign to me, because I've found very little mystery and a marked lack of evil capitalistic conspiracies at the top. In fact, most CEOs are people basically like yourself—with perhaps an intensification of certain important personal traits. In expressing such an opinion, I realize I could be accused of bias. But perhaps as we explore a few of the activities and personal qualities of those at the top, you'll understand there's a solid empirical basis for my positive viewpoint.

For example, take the process of *choosing* a chief executive officer. There is usually nothing very dramatic that happens when a person moves into the top spot in a company. In most cases, about three to six people are known to be leading candidates, and there may be some mild surprise if one is chosen over the others. But big shocks are the exception, because more CEOs have risen gradually from other jobs in the corporation, and most of the company's top officers know from personal experience what the company needs in the person of a chief executive officer at a particular time and also what specific individual is most likely to fulfill that need.

When the company management has reached the point where it's about to name a new CEO, the outgoing CEO has probably been in his position for about ten years. During the period of his tenure, there may be as many as fifteen or so officers who appear to be CEO material. As a preliminary informal screening process, which is related as much to the current performance of their duties as to their possible elevation to a higher position in the future, these people may go in for private interviews with the incumbent CEO. In these sessions, they may be asked to give their views about what the future direction of the company should be and how they might handle certain organizational problems if they should arise.

Then, as the abilities of these top officers become clearer, certain tentative decisions start to be made as to how they may fit into the corporate organization in future years. As I said, about three to six of these people will eventually be chosen as possibilities to fill the top slot in the company. But a "change of command" often requires a shifting and reorganization in other jobs in the company's upper echelons of management as well. So the selection of a new CEO isn't just a matter of moving a new person in at the top and moving his predecessor out. Rather, it's often a complex refitting of a new corporate jigsaw puzzle.

The final step of choosing the top officer is rather methodical and straightforward, and the selection is made much like any other major company decision. The last few moves a person makes at the top of his company are determined by fewer and fewer people, because, by definition, there are progressively fewer bosses above you.

In most cases, the CEO himself makes the final recommendation on his successor, and then the board of directors makes it official. Most people who qualify for consideration for the top job have demonstrated success at running a particular division of the company. Or perhaps they have moved up steadily with a high performance rating through the progressive offices of vice-president, senior vice-president, executive vice-president, and president—with chairman of the board, or CEO, being the only office they haven't held.

Among the people I know who have made it to the very top, only a few are what you would classify as geniuses. Most seem to have a basic intelligence that's above average, but intelligence is just one of several key factors. I have observed people of superior intelligence who were smarter than their bosses—and I suspect you have too. It takes mental agility, but also much more, to function at the highest levels of most corporations. What I'd like to do now is give you some personal impressions about what that "something more" is.

I should mention at the outset that I'm not going to try to come up with a definitive profile of the typical chief executive officer. I really don't think there *is* any such profile, because there are almost as many different kinds of personalities at the top as you'll find walking down a busy street in any American city. But I have noticed a few common features that characterize these divergent leaders at the top.

Here are a few of them:

First of all, these individuals have a *high level of self-control and self-discipline*. If one of them tells you he's going to do something, you can depend on his following through with it in the time frame you've agreed upon. Most of the CEOs I know lead quite regular lives, too. They don't try to burn the candle at both ends by partying until the wee hours and then attempting to do an efficient day's work on three or four hours' sleep.

In my career, I've run into many people who simply don't know when to go home from a social gathering or when to put down a thriller and turn out the lights. And then there are the TV addicts who absolutely *have* to watch a late movie on the tube two or three times a week—because it's a "classic" or for some other transparent rationalization.

Now, I realize it's dangerous to generalize about habits like this, because some people can function on very little sleep. But for most of us, it's necessary to be certain that we get at least six to eight hours a night if we hope to function at top form. People who live by undisciplined daily schedules may rise fairly high in a company just because they're strong in a particular field. But they could be much more effective and alert in doing their routine work and rendering tough business judgments if they would learn a little self-control.

Excessive work can sometimes be as much a culprit in destroying your efficiency as too much partying or TV. So most top executives seem to know when to call it a day and head for home. I'm not suggesting that these top people don't work hard, because they do. In fact, I'm not sure it's possible to work too hard, so long as you don't encroach too much on your family life or your sleep. I'm just saying that the majority of senior executives have ordered their lives in such a way that they produce at the maximum level at which they are capable of producing—without going overboard and hurting their bodies or human relationships.

It's interesting to note in this regard that in a recent survey by the Gallup Poll and the *Wall Street Journal* of the wives of top executives from 1,300 of the largest U.S. companies, 80 percent of the women said they had been married for twenty years or longer. In a related finding, a 1980 Arthur Young & Company study revealed that fewer than 3 percent at the time of the survey were divorced or separated, and none were single or widowed. In contrast, nearly 20 percent of all American males between the ages of forty-five and seventy were unmarried at the time the Arthur Young survey was conducted.

Of course, statistics like these don't say anything about the *quality* of the marital relationships among the nation's top corporate officers. As a matter of fact, in the Gallup–*Wall Street Journal* survey, many of the wives of executives indicated a significant number of pressures and personal problems. But at the same time, many of these executive marriages have at least hung together and, in fact, would be regarded as reasonably successful by most standards. So I would conclude that despite their hard work and long hours, many CEOs regard their family lives as important enough not to slight or ignore them in their upward climb.

Another key characteristic of the typical chief executive officers I know is that they *communicate well at every level in the company*. A large number of executives surveyed by Korn/Ferry International said that "getting along with others or human relations" was the biggest single factor in their success. This factor ranked third, behind "hard work" and "ambition/drive/desire to achieve."

It's also extremely important that the person at the top of a company be a good communicator with those in positions *below* him so that he will be able to gather as much information as possible for each decision he must make. The executive who tends to intimidate people or doesn't listen well to them is seriously handicapped in his advancement to the top because he has failed to encourage or even permit good staff communications.

Another very important quality, which I've mentioned before but which gains increasing importance at the top, is a *sense of humor*. The reason it's so essential for the top man to be able occasionally to see something humorous in his business is that his attitude tends to set the tone for the company as a whole. Humor sometimes breaks feelings of tension in serious discussions and enables people to approach a subject more objectively. You simply can't be at your best if you're tense.

So if a boss can't laugh at matters that have a genuinely funny side to them, his staff will immediately label him as a person with no sense of humor. That kind of reputation may well increase the stress level among the boss's closest associates. And the somber, overly serious mood will tend to sift down and affect the company at lower levels as well.

An additional feature I've noticed in many top executives is an *emphasis on health and physical fitness*. It's hard to be an alcoholic or drink excessive amounts of coffee daily and still be in the best condition to make measured, calm, thoughtful decisions. Also, it helps to devote some time each week to exercise, both to relax and also to keep your circulation moving. Most of the high-level people I know get some sort of regular exercise, whether through athletics or a structured fitness program.

A large proportion of corporate officers love to compete in sports, and although they're not bad losers, they are all tough competitors, real tigers who love to win. They love the opportunity to unwind physically, mix with gregarious, active people, and test their physical skills against those of others.

Another important quality in a top executive is the *ability to think abstractly and conceptually so that you can see the "big picture,"* or the key issue involved in a particular problem or situation. To put this another way, it's important for the head of a company to be able to go directly through complex material and get to the heart of a matter as quickly and efficiently as possible.

And this quality can sometimes encourage a final important characteristic in chief executive officers — a *willingness to take significant risks* that could affect their careers. If you have thoroughly conceptualized a problem, or thought your way completely through it so that you understand all its implications, that process can lead you to a conclusion that will involve a calculated business gamble—a risk that you might never have considered without such serious thought and study.

Now let me illustrate both this "big picture" mentality and the risking-taking quality that can result from it by referring to an incident from my own experience.

Most people who have commented on my movement up in the Penney Company have cited some work I did in the corporation's catalog division as the key to my becoming chief executive officer. We entered the catalog business back in 1963, and I got involved as the director of that division in 1964.

Most companies already in the catalog business had started more or less the same way. They had begun their catalog sales programs on a small scale, and they had eventually grown very large over a period of years. For a number of reasons, we wanted to shorten the growth period. We wanted to *start out big*—that was the *concept* we elected to try.

But there were also significant risks. By making the decision to put out a full-blown, 1,200-page catalog at the outset, we committed ourselves to high initial fixed costs. The strategy was to develop a large customer base in a relatively short time so that we could quickly develop enough of a sales base to offset the high fixed costs. The risk lay in the uncertainty as to our ability actually to build this large customer base quickly.

In the catalog business, you have high fixed costs that leverage against you at lower sales volumes, but leverage for you at a high sales volume. Since the variable costs tend to be relatively low throughout, you can achieve quite high profits if you can quickly get your sales volume up to a reasonably high level.

The uncharted part of all this is that, to my knowledge, nobody had ever done this before: Nobody had ever gone into the catalog business on a large scale at the outset with anything as big as a 1,200-page catalog, and also immediately built the huge support facilities to back it up.

So the pressure built up on me and my staff as we had

to make recommendations about how to move ahead. After sifting through all the cost analyses and other data, we decided on an approach, and the top-level officers in the company bought the proposal. At that point, they put themselves on the line too, and their personal risks became at least as great as ours.

We had settled on setting up a small network of large, automated, computer-driven distribution centers around the country. We had an advantage over our competition because we were entering the business rather late and weren't encumbered by the old ways of operating or by outdated equipment. But because our fixed costs would be very high in building one of these plants, it was essential that all our projections and background information be as accurate as possible to increase our chances for success.

I felt rather confident when we embarked on planning the first of our distribution centers, just outside Atlanta. We began to sustain the initial huge operating losses we had expected in the first couple of years as we incurred our large initial fixed costs. And I knew that some of my friends and other company officers who were entitled to share in corporate profits were privately calculating the effect this project was having on their personal compensation. I imagined they were whispering in frustration, "What are those catalog people doing down there?"

But everything was proceeding according to schedule, and I wasn't at all worried — at least not until I went down to Atlanta for an on-site inspection. We approached the building site from the rear and parked behind a clump of trees; as a result, I couldn't see anything at first. But when I stepped out from behind the trees onto the side of a hill that overlooked the rising distribution center, I was stunned. In fact, my stomach did such a flip-flop I thought I was going to be ill.

Out below me, like some great Cecil B. De Mille extravaganza, the distribution center was rising from the ground, a huge steel structure that covered fifty-two acres on a man-made plateau. The building would house more than two million square feet of working space — and would be the largest continuous roof in the United States at that time. Needless to say, I felt tremendous personal responsibility for the project.

"This could become one of the largest monuments in the world to somebody's mistake," I muttered to myself as we walked down to the building area.

But the more I saw of the plant, the more excited I got. My colleagues and I knew that the potential was there and that the information and projections we had gathered were the best available. There were definite risks—for the company and for the people involved as well. If the project failed, the company would not only lose a great deal of money, but its management reputation would suffer. And I would probably face considerable damage to my own reputation as a manager.

As it happened, our predictions about success turned out to be conservative. We had projected that the catalog division would show a profit by 1972, but we reached that goal a year ahead of time, in 1971.

You never know exactly what the final results of your current tasks and achievements will be, and I certainly didn't enter that catalog project with the idea of aiming toward my present job a decade or more in advance. But I would encourage you, when you're offered a big responsibility that carries certain risks, to consider going ahead with it and not to back off just because some possible hazards to your career are involved.

So, if you hope to move up to the highest management levels, learn to gather all the facts, analyze what they mean, weigh the risks and rewards, and then move ahead. If you take this approach and the opportunity arises for you to head a big project or make a decision that changes the course of your company for the better, you'll be in a much better position to move up.

These, then, are a few of the qualities that have impressed me about people I know who have become chief executive officers. But I wouldn't by any means want to leave you with the impression that I think the characteristics are written in concrete.

I know a number of top executives whose personalities and careers don't fit into this mold at all. But I also know that having some of these features in your personal makeup won't hurt you, and they may very well help. There are no perfect stereotypes of the "man at the top," but at the same time, there are certain common strengths that I would encourage you to cultivate if you have ambitions for higher office. And when you come right down to it, these qualities — self-control, a communications ability, a sense of humor, personal health, and a flair for creative conceptualizing and risk-taking—tend to make you not only a better executive, but a better person as well.

You may be promoted in part because you are an intelligent and productive worker, but you'll also be more likely to move up if your bosses believe you're a good model for those you are supervising. Every time they promote you, they are in effect saying to your peers and subordinates, "This person possesses the qualities we'd like to see in more of our workers."

If you can meet that standard of leadership in your corporation now and continue to live up to it as you rise from one level to the next, you'll probably find more doors of opportunity swinging open to ever higher positions.

CHAPTER 14
YOUR SILENT PARTNERS

As you move up to the higher levels in your company, there are two sets of "support systems" that become increasingly important — your family and your inner resources. We've already explored these two areas at different points in this book, but I want to devote some time now to a few additional personal observations about how your family, your close friends, and your value system can interact to provide a solid undergirding for your business life.

First of all, let's consider your family — or more specifically, a family concern that has come to the fore in recent years as more women have moved into the workplace. I'm referring to the personal issues and problems raised by the two-career family, in which both the husband and wife hold down full-time jobs and harbor ambitions to move as high as possible in their chosen fields.

As I see it, this two-career issue may be the most important that many working people will have to confront in future years. One or both spouses will have to decide whether they are willing to accept second-best in their careers in order to keep their family intact and preserve marital harmony. If a person is ambitious and also puts a high value on a stable family life, this issue can create tremendous personal pressures.

For example, if a husband and wife both work for the

Penney Company, and one is offered the job of managing a store in a single-store market in which we wouldn't be able to find a job for the other spouse, that would present some serious personal and career problems. From the company side, we are becoming more sensitive to this sort of situation. But the solutions often aren't easy and usually do require some degree of compromise on the part of one or both spouses.

A sensitive boss would probably, at a minimum, at least bring the two married workers in (if they worked for the same company) and ask, "We are considering one of you for a move. Will that create a problem for your family?" Then he'd pursue the discussion and try to determine if there was some way to arrive at a workable plan for both.

There are few guidelines in this area right now, and mistakes are bound to be made and feelings hurt. Still, there are some things that need to be said about this issue of the two-career couple. In the ensuing comments, I'll be relying on my own personal observations, and also on information and impressions I've gained as chairman of Catalyst, an organization that specializes in researching the challenges facing working women.

First of all, it's important to understand what is meant by a "two-career marriage." The main assumption behind this concept is that *both* spouses are career-oriented. They both want to move up in their companies or professions as far as their talents will take them. If only one of the spouses is focusing on a career with this intensity, and the other, while holding down a part-time or even full-time job, is not upwardly mobile in a career sense, then you don't have a two-career family. Rather, you have a family in which both spouses work, but only one is career-oriented.

In many marriages today, you have what might be

called a "traditional" working-couple situation, in which the husband is the one who is career-oriented. The wife, on the other hand, holds down a job that may bring in important extra income to help defray household expenses. But there is a clear-cut assumption made by both spouses that the husband's job is more important. As a result, if he has to move to another part of the country to follow a job opportunity, then she will quit her job and try to find something else in their new location.

But the rules of the game change when both spouses are career-oriented. In that case, the careers of husband and wife are more likely to be regarded as equal in importance, and the decisions about whether or not to relocate in order to move up in a company can't be made as easily.

Needless to say, there are many problems involved in making a two-career marriage work. In many cases, there aren't any easy answers, and the most effective solutions tend to come from the individuals involved, rather than from some pundit's general pronouncement about what is the right or wrong thing to do in every situation. So I'm more concerned here with pointing out some of the major questions you should be asking yourself if you're involved in a two-career marriage, rather than with trying to present any definitive solutions. Here, then, are a few of the questions that you might consider:

1. *What are your priorities in your career and family life?* I'm a great believer in the principle of putting your family before your job. But sometimes that principle can be obscured by the time and energy demands of a high-powered, upwardly mobile career. If your family really is very important to you, then you must consciously plan time to spend with your spouse and children. Otherwise, it's likely that they'll end up with little or none of your attention.

2. *What should be your philosophy about having children?* Some two-career couples have decided that their work is so important that children don't have any place in their lives, and so they have elected to remain childless. That's certainly a possible solution, but many other couples I meet fall into the category of "wanting it all." In other words, they want a full career *and* a full family life. And therein lie many of the stresses and strains of the two-career marriage.

First of all, I don't think there is any one correct answer as to whether a couple should have children early in their careers, before they get too fixed on a track to the upper levels of management, or later, after they are more established professionally. But this is certainly an important question to consider, and each couple will have to grapple with it before they embark on starting a family.

Another key issue that the two-career couple must face is the question of whether the mother or father should take a lengthy maternity or paternity leave. In other words, should one spouse just quit full-time work for a few months or even years to devote more extensive time to child-rearing, perhaps until the youngsters are of school age? Or should the couple hire a governess to handle most of the daily tasks of bringing up the kids?

No matter what decision you make in the abstract before the baby arrives, you may well find yourselves making some adjustments and perhaps even radical changes after the birth actually occurs. For example, I know of a number of cases in which a career-oriented woman had resolved to take off work for a month and then return to her job. But maternal (and paternal) feelings aren't always that easy to control, and sometimes the new mother simply can't bring herself to leave her child almost completely in the care of a baby-sitter. In other cases, a parent may plan to take off to care for the baby, but then the loss of that extra income makes the financial situation too tight — and back to work goes the child-caring spouse.

3. *Should you get involved in long-range commuting?* There have been a number of articles written recently about couples who are living apart from one another, in different cities, so that they can pursue separate careers. Typically, they keep in touch regularly by long-distance phone calls and "commute" back and forth on weekends to spend at least a couple of days a week together.

I must say I am quite sympathetic to this problem, because I was separated from my wife and family for more than three years early in my career when I was serving as a district manager for Penney. I would be gone from Sunday night or Monday morning until Friday night every week for most of that period.

In some ways, that was the equivalent of modern-day long-range commuting, and there are definitely potential problems with this style of life. If one parent is on the road or out of the city most of the time, he or she may lose many opportunities to spend time with the kids — and to nurture a good relationship with the other parent. If *both* parents travel a great deal, the children may become the responsibility of a full-time baby-sitter. Then, when there are discipline problems, accidents, and important issues that arise in school, one or both parents may miss the opportunity to have a say in important decisions affecting the child's development.

Then there may be other problems when you come home on the weekends with limited time to spend with your children, and you want it to be pleasant. But too often, there may be an accumulation of problems that your spouse feels you should resolve, such as determining a punishment. Another difficulty is that if you only have weekends to devote to your family, you have to divide a severely limited amount of time between your kids and your spouse. It's rather hard to join your son or daughter at an athletic contest, take your spouse out to dinner, tie up the loose ends of family business, and still have a relaxed time on your two days off.

But with proper planning, many of these problems in a long-distance relationship can be minimized. If you find that for a certain assignment you have to be away during the week and can get home only on weekends, it's quite possible to decide in advance how you're going to schedule your relationship with your children and your spouse. Then, if you give them the best of yourself during the couple of days you're at home, you may find that you're developing a better relationship with them than many of your "stay-at-home" colleagues are with their families. If a person is always hiding behind a newspaper, sitting in front of a television set, or otherwise ignoring his family, he might as well be living in another city seven days a week!

4. *What should you do if one spouse has a chance to relocate to another part of the country?* One way to handle this problem is, obviously, for the two-career couple to commute long-distance between two cities. But suppose the husband and wife find this solution unacceptable? What then?

I think the key principle here is communication—first between husband and wife, and then between each of them and his or her company management. These days, most large companies are sensitive to this problem and will try to do what they can to help, such as delay a move for a brief period or help the spouse to relocate at the other end. Companies may also offer professional job counseling or actually make positions available for both spouses.

But, again, I think early communications and measured, cautious decision-making are the most important things to focus on here. Before you accept an early transfer too quickly or turn it down before you find out whether it really may work, be absolutely sure you discuss the matter in depth not only with your spouse but also with your company management!

5. *If you're near the beginning of your career, should you and your spouse consider future job patterns that will be more "flexible" or "portable"?* In other words, should you look for work that will perhaps afford each of you the ability to move about more freely when unexpected opportunities arise in the other's job? This is a difficult question, but one which many young two-career couples are considering seriously.

Here's one pertinent case that was called to my attention recently by Liz Roman Gallese, a business writer based in New York City:

One young man, age thirty-two, seemed much the type of person American corporations want most to attract: prep school, Princeton, Harvard Business School, the Navy.

But he turned down a top offer from a big engineering company in Pittsburgh after graduation, even though he was favored by a key member of top management. At the "Big Eight" accounting firm he did join in Chicago, he refused two transfers — to New York and Washington, D.C. — in his four-year tenure that could have assured partnership.

Finally, he left the accounting firm for a small consulting company that above all offers the type of "flexibility" he has to have, such as the option of setting up his office in another city if necessary or of choosing his own clients to cut down on travel.

The reason: his wife.

She, too, at age twenty-nine, is a graduate of Harvard Business School, and she is currently on a fast track in marketing at a Fortune 500 company. It will only be a matter of time, he predicts, before she accepts a transfer for promotion or gets an offer she can't refuse from a firm miles away from Chicago.

"Two M.B.A.s have to foresee problems," he says. "Companies don't understand the problems of dual-career professionals."

Another way this couple is attempting to plan ahead is that they are hedging their bets by launching their own company during their off-hours. Over the past three years, they've spent $15,000 of their own money, used up vacation time, and worked nights and weekends— often laying plans and plotting strategies over dinner at a suburban Chinese restaurant.

Both husband and wife say they haven't abandoned their respective consulting and corporate careers. But just in case they face problems in the future, and just in case their venture does take off, well then, "It is another option, another iron in the fire," she says.

It's true that there are some fields or specialties that enable people to change locations more easily than others, and this two-career couple is attempting with some apparent success to find their own solution to this problem of career "flexibility." Other more "portable" jobs include consulting, engineering, "in-house" corporate law, and other professional skills. But sometimes it's difficult or even impossible to be so selective when a person is looking for a good job. When the best initial career opportunity requires you to focus on one company or industry, it could be more difficult to relocate. And the question of trying to develop a "flexible" career pattern may become academic after you've already established yourself on an "inflexible" but still promising upward track in some corporation.

6. *How should you divide household chores?* This may seem a rather humble, unimportant topic to consider in the midst of all the exotic issues that can arise with a two-career family. But I think it's an important thing for *all* couples to resolve.

First of all, if both spouses are working at well-paying jobs, they may be able to hire someone to do some of the housekeeping chores. But there are *always* some things, perhaps involving work around the house or caring for the children, that will demand some time. And if one spouse ends up doing all this household work, the result will probably be detrimental for the entire family.

I have a personal view on this matter: I think that both spouses should share household chores, no matter how hard one or the other works in an office. I don't expect to cook dinner when I get home, but I do expect to clear off the table and help with the dishes. We don't have much time for a leisurely evening together anyway, and if I go off somewhere and read the paper while Verna does the dishes, that will be that much less time that we are together.

If we do the dishes together, we save fifteen or twenty minutes, and we're together while we're doing this household chore. The way I see it, there's no such thing as men's work and women's work. And whoever is available should do it, especially if joint work provides more "togetherness time."

7. *Are you prepared for one spouse to be more success-ful than the other?* Even as I ask this question, I'm really not sure that most ambitious people can prepare them-selves for their spouse to be more successful than they are. Dual-career couples will inevitably have to grapple with the question of how they handle a sense of competi-tion between themselves. But I don't think there is any one solution to this problem that will work for every couple, or even most couples.

I can think of wives who earn more than their hus-bands do, even though in some cases when the couple started out, his salary was higher than hers. Sometimes the wife's job is higher on the executive ladder and more demanding in terms of time commitments. She's the one who has to work late many nights and attend Saturday meetings. The husband can easily become resentful in this sort of situation.

There are serious problems here involving ego, level of personal maturity, and the importance of inner achievement orientations. The only way I can see to deal with the success issue successfully is for the couple to get it out on the table early in their relationship and talk about it before bad feelings begin to fester and erode the relationship.

These, then, are just a few of the questions that might be raised to help the dual-career couple avoid problems in their relationship before they arise. But underlying this entire discussion is another issue—the question of developing a mutual value system.

For a spouse to operate at his or her maximum effec-tiveness at work or in any other "extra-family" activity, I believe it's extremely important for both the husband and wife to affirm the same general set of personal values and then to grow together in that value system over a lifetime. Having the same general goals and priorities with respect to child-rearing, money management, charitable giving, and personal service to others can eliminate many problems before they even appear.

This kind of common foundation at home also provides an invaluable base from which to operate most effectively in the outside world. Of course, I realize that a husband and wife may never agree completely on what is ultimately important in life and what's not. But the closer you and your spouse can grow in this dimension of your lives, the stronger you'll find yourself becoming at work.

It's possible to get the same kind of support from the children, too, if you'll just find a way to work them into your busy schedule. I know people who actually schedule time with their spouses and children, and they stick to those appointments as faithfully as they would to a meeting with the President of the United States. They reap the bountiful rewards of this kind of commitment, too, as they find their kids supporting them in their jobs and even offering them spiritual comfort.

But all this takes time. You have to organize your day so that you're available to interact with your spouse and children on these deeper levels. It won't do to plan to see your son or daughter or spouse in a larger group of people. You have to deal with each of them in one-to-one encounters and conversations.

In addition to support from your family, you might also be interested in seeking a similar kind of encouragement from other people in the business world. In this regard, it may be worthwhile to start some sort of "value-focus" group to discuss goals or problems in light of the particular personal philosophy or religious orientation you have affirmed. Such outlets can be particularly helpful for unmarried people who may lack close family ties.

For me, this has meant getting involved in a small group in which I have an opportunity to do some Bible study and then spend some time talking and praying with my peers over personal concerns that may be on my mind. Specifically, I meet with Bill Kanaga, chairman of Arthur Young & Company, and Howard Kauffmann, president of Exxon. We try to meet once a week at 7:00 a.m. for about an hour. But as a practical matter, we may get together only about three times a month because of our packed schedules and frequent business trips. We follow a Bible-study program put out by the Navigators organization, and we move very slowly through the outline, because practical personal and business topics, sometimes with spiritual and moral implications, frequently pop up in our discussions.

For example, one of us might be trying to decide whether to accept an invitation to give a commencement address at a local university. We would then discuss whatever issues are involved and pray for wisdom for the person making the decision. Or there might have been an article in a newspaper about some alleged payoffs involving one of our companies, and we would give the person concerned some moral support as he wrestled with a decision on the problem. We also share family problems and other personal concerns that may be bothering us.

One thing we do *not* do during these sessions, however, is discuss confidential matters involving our companies. If the problem has made the newspapers or otherwise become known, we feel free to discuss the public information. But each of us has many confidential relationships to maintain back in his own office, and we have an implied understanding that we don't share those confidences with each other.

Of course, that doesn't mean we can't pray about an undisclosed problem. We just don't feel free to give the details about what those problems involve. For example, I might say to the other two men, "I'm facing a tough decision today in the office, and I'd like you to pray that I'll have the wisdom necessary to make the right choice." A prayer under these circumstances can be tremendously effective, and yet does not have to violate any proprietary information in my company.

Also, even though we may not get specific about a certain problem we're facing just when it comes up, we've had enough general discussions on business morality and ethics over the years in this group to give one another an extremely helpful foundation for making wiser business decisions. Our study of the Bible and moral principles relating to business situations gives us a wealth of knowledge about how to deal with ethical issues on the job.

These sessions are particularly effective in reinforcing the personal values that each of us has affirmed in his life. It's hard, if not impossible, to spend some time sharpening your ethical sensitivities in an intense sharing experience like this, and then to go right out and violate the very principles you've been espousing.

I'm certainly not saying that this type of value-focus group is an essential prerequisite to becoming a good upper-level executive or chief executive officer. But I've found it to be an extremely useful undergirding for my own business life, and I know of a number of other such groups that serve similar functions on lower management levels.

As a matter of fact, these small groups are found in most of the big cities in our country. But it's impossible to keep track of exactly how many there are and where they meet because there's often no umbrella organization that sets them up and keeps tabs on them. If you're interested in starting a group like this, here are a few guidelines I've found helpful:

—Keep the group small, say three to six people. Two probably won't give you enough of a variety of opinions, but more than about six may make those participating reluctant to share on a deep level unless they all know each other very well before they get started.

—The participants should all make generally the same basic value assumptions. In my group, we're all Christians, and we all assume that the Bible is our primary source of spiritual authority. If one of us didn't take the Bible very seriously, we might spend most of our time arguing about the basic ground rules that should guide us, rather than dealing with the pressing practical problems we confront at work every day.

—Those involved should probably come from different companies or be on a relatively equal, noncompetitive level in the same company. If you're trying to pray and share personal concerns with a superior or subordinate in your own department, it can be extremely difficult to be open and honest. There's always a tendency for the boss and his employee to worry just how a certain idea or thought may be interpreted. So it's best to avoid that difficulty altogether if you can.

In my own case, I feel most comfortable relating in a value-focus group to other top executives outside my own company because I know there will be no problems with personality dynamics within the corporate hierarchy. Also, I know these individuals can understand the problems I'm facing because they have similar concerns themselves.

These are just a few of the guidelines that our group

has found helpful, but you might think of some others that would be necessary for any group you would want to join. In any case, there are no hard-and-fast rules for this sort of thing.

You may wonder whether a reliance some people place on such groups is entirely healthy. I've heard some skeptics ask: "Isn't it better just to try to become independent and rely entirely on yourself and your own resources to solve your problems, rather than on other people?"

I agree it's important to develop an independent, secure inner core to your personality if you hope to move up in business. But human beings are not little islands who function best in a vacuum. No, we're basically social creatures. We need input from other people to realize our full potential.

As an executive, I know I make better decisions when I have a full array of facts and advice from my staff and colleagues. Similarly, I know I can function better in a more *personal* sense and can develop deeper reservoirs of inner strength if I get some help from others on that level.

So these "silent partners" in your work, including sympathetic friends and family members, can provide you with a supportive foundation for accomplishing something significant in the world of business. They may not work beside you and may have no direct say in whether you get the next promotion that comes along. But the strength they can inject into your life may be more valuable in the long run for your career than all the business guidance you could glean from any corporate colleague or mentor.

CHAPTER 15

SHARING SUCCESS

Some of the unhappiest people I know are those who work toward a big career goal, achieve it, and then expect to live happily ever after by "hoarding" their success.

Perhaps they concentrate all their energies on trying to parlay their career position into some lofty social standing. Or they may just accumulate mounds of material goods and investments and expect the resulting creature comforts to keep them completely content with life. But it never works.

The only kind of success that means anything involves achieving a goal and then sharing that achievement with others in some way— in terms of both time and money. Let me give you a few examples to illustrate what I mean.

A great deal has been written in recent years about "simple living" and paring down excessive spending so that you can have more to give away to others who are less fortunate. An early model for this approach to simple living was the founder of Methodism, John Wesley. In some years, he earned as much as 1,400 English pounds from the sales of his books—a handsome sum in those days. But he continued to live on only thirty pounds and gave the difference away.

He wrote, "If I leave behind me ten pounds, you and all mankind bear witness against me that I lived and died a thief and a robber." And he seems to have managed substantially to have fulfilled this vow, because when he did die, his possessions consisted of two silver spoons, an old frock coat, and a silver teapot.

Now, I'm certainly not suggesting that I expect everybody to be quite as generous with his worldly goods as Wesley was. Frankly, I don't think I know anybody who is quite the model of charity that he seems to have been. But I do believe his life has some important lessons for those who are moving up in their corporate hierarchy and getting higher and higher compensation for their services.

First of all, I believe that greater power and responsibility in your business necessarily carry greater responsibilities to the people you work with and also to the community at large. Some of our worldly goods obviously have to be spent in satisfying our own needs. But we also have an obligation to share some of our material goods with those who are less fortunate. The more successful we become, the greater the responsibility we have to share our relative abundance—in both material and experiential terms—with the society that has made our success possible.

The second thing that Wesley's life says to me is that it's a compelling idea to affirm a limited style of living— one that will satisfy your needs but isn't necessarily tied down to the amount of money you make. Then, rather than expanding your personal expenditures as your income expands, you might put increasing amounts of your money into worthwhile projects in the community at large.

These may appear to be rather radical suggestions, especially if you and your family have been scrimping to keep up with high prices on what may seem a relatively low middle manager's salary. When you finally find yourself making considerably more in the upper management levels in your company, the temptation may be to decide, "I worked hard to get where I am, and I'm not about to share what I'm earning with anybody except those who are closest to me!"

But I've become convinced that this sort of attitude is a trap. If you hoard the fruits of your success, you'll rob yourself of great inner contentment that can come as you reach out and help others who may not have been quite as lucky as you in moving up the ladder. A gift to a poor person or a good charity such as the United Way or a church or synagogue does more than just enhance the well-being of another individual or organization. Your contribution actually becomes a kind of investment you're making in the community at large — an investment that will bring back returns in personal satisfaction and goodwill that you never even imagined when you first made the gift.

Also, by giving to worthy causes and needy individuals, you'll be placing yourself firmly in the long-standing American tradition of volunteerism—a tradition which has recently been reasserting itself in the wake of federal cutbacks in social-welfare programs. There is a greater need now than at any time in the recent past for relatively successful individuals to commit themselves to sharing greater portions of their material rewards.

But now let me offer a few words of caution and qualification. First of all, I'm not suggesting that it's a good idea to look for some doctrinaire, across-the-board application of any of these sharing principles for your own life. Each person's circumstances are different, and so there is probably some special way of arranging your own style of living and giving that would be appropriate for you and for no one else.

Also, I'm not suggesting in the course of this discussion that I think there's something wrong with earning a big salary. Nor am I saying that I feel there's something wrong with living fairly comfortably or saving for retirement. Some simple-living advocates have implied that there's something inherently wrong with making a lot of money, but I'm afraid I just can't buy that approach. The important thing, it seems to me, is not so much how much you make as what you do with it.

In stressing the importance of sharing your success with others, though, I wouldn't want to leave the impression that I think this sharing involves only money or material things. As we've already seen, an executive's time is in many ways the most valuable commodity he has to offer—and the thing he's least willing to give up. It's much easier to give a donation to a local college than it is to go out there and deliver a talk on the business world to a group of students. Yet the school and the students may get much more out of your sharing of your experiences with them than they will out of your gift of money.

The further up the corporate ladder you move, the more wisdom and advice you have to offer younger people. You may think you don't have anything to share at all; but think back on yourself five or ten or more years ago. If you had known then what you know now, you would be a great deal better off, wouldn't you?

No matter how little you think you know or have to offer, there are many who can benefit from your experience. Furthermore, I believe each of us, at various levels of achievement in business, has a responsibility to share what he knows with those on lower levels. Taking the initiative to help those below you—including students who haven't even entered the working world — will strengthen the entire business system. And the very act of giving your time away to others will strengthen you too, both because of the inner satisfaction you'll get from giving a helping hand to another human being, and because of mental sharpening you'll experience yourself as you respond to others' questions.

In many ways, success in the business world is a cyclical thing in which one person moves up toward the top and then, in a sense, goes back to the bottom again by reaching down from his position of strength and helping others to make their way up the corporate ladder. I could never have made it to the position I occupy today without the patience and instruction of others. And the other chief executive officers I know are equally indebted to many helping hands along the way. When you've received assistance, you are immediately confronted with the responsibility of giving assistance.

But this process of helping and sharing is not some onerous obligation or some one-way street that results in aid to the other person but nothing to you. You shouldn't set out to give away your money or time or influence only with an eye to what you're going to get in return. But if you give freely, you have every reason to expect a good "return on your investment" in the form of personal satisfaction—and perhaps even greater material benefits.

I've known many people who have spent vast amounts of time or money on a particular person or project without any expectation of getting anything in return. They gave out of the goodness of their hearts, and weren't even looking for a thank-you. Yet weeks, months, or even years later the person or organization they helped crossed their path again and returned the original gifts they had given many times over. In a number of cases, that unexpected return on investment came from a staff person who strengthened the entire organization and played a key role in a later promotion of the executive who had originally provided the help.

There is a fundamental principle of human relationships operating here which I don't pretend to understand. But I know it works, and I know it has something to do with the message a man from Galilee uttered so many years ago: ". . . give and it will be given to you; good measure, pressed down, shaken together, running over, will be put into your lap. For the measure you give will be the measure you get back" (Luke 6:38, RSV).